MAIN EVENT

Roberta Morgan

MAIN EVENT

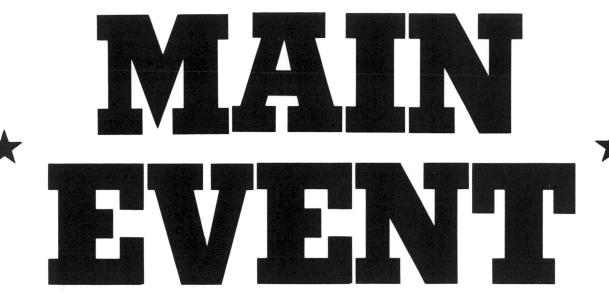

★ ★

★

The World of Professional Wrestling

The Dial Press   New York

Published by
The Dial Press
1 Dag Hammarskjold Plaza
New York, New York 10017

Manufactured in the United States of America

First printing

Design by Francesca Belanger

Library of Congress Cataloging in Publication Data

Morgan, Roberta, 1953–
Main event.

Includes index.
1. Wrestling.   I. Title.
GV1195.M67   796.8′12   79-362
ISBN 0-8037-5631-3
ISBN 0-8037-5633-3 pbk.

For Belle, Bernard, and Brian

Acknowledgments

In a book of this kind very little can be accomplished without a lot of help. Therefore I would like to thank warmly the following people, who gave their time and effort to make this book a reality.

David Landsman, whose countless hours of travel and research made everything possible and tied everything together; Britt Bell, a great editor, who believed in this book and in the sport from the very start. Lou Sahadi, for helping, advising, and sharing with me his vast experience from more than 15 years of involvement with professional wrestling. George Napolitano and Frank Amato, for their outstanding photographs of action in the ring.

The officials, managers, promoters, administrators, referees, and personnel of the World Wide Wrestling Federation, the National Wrestling Alliance, and the American Wrestling Association—their help is more than I can describe, their friendship and courtesy the key to all the work done.

Tom Burke, of Global Wrestling, for his aid and information throughout, especially for the tag team chapter and historical background.

The wrestlers, who took their time before and after matches to speak with me and who showed always what true professionals they are.

And the fans, without whom there would be nothing . . .

★ Contents ★

★ *Introduction* ★

"The Greatest Spectator Sport in the World"

He had him in what was obviously a choke hold, though the referee could not see it. I knew that an object was clenched in his fist and as he landed a jab to the throat, I saw the man I was rooting for fall to the canvas in agony. His opponent then landed a kick to the midsection, then another, and another, and the fallen man doubled up in pain. His attacker picked him up and pulled him over to the buckle, first tearing away the protective covering and then ramming his head into the exposed metal of the cornerpost. Blood covered his face. I could hardly speak. His opponent then backed away and turned around to face the crowd, raising his arm in triumph. All of a sudden, the grinning victor was lifted high into the air and brought crashing down to the mat. I held my breath as the referee counted . . . one . . . two . . . three. The pin was made. We had won!

Annual attendance at wrestling matches in the United States is estimated at between 25 and 30 million. There are wrestling matches all over the country, every day of the year. Millions more watch wrestling on television, as many or more than watch the Super Bowl, and in some areas of the

country wrestling is on television every night of the week. There are dozens of wrestling magazines, all with healthy circulations. Wrestling matches in Madison Square Garden draw capacity crowds of 22,000—even

Ivan Koloff (*top*) vs. Mil Mascaras (*George Napolitano*)

INTRODUCTION

26,000 when the match is broadcast on closed-circuit TV in the adjoining Felt Forum—and that figure does not include the fans turned away from the gates! The *New York Post* claimed that the attendance at a recent match was the largest for any event of any kind ever held in the Garden. Outside the United States professional wrestling has a large and loyal following in Japan, Europe, Australia, New Zealand, and South Africa.

So, no getting away from it, professional wrestling is one of the most popular, if not the most popular, spectator sport in the world. To invoke this sort of loyalty, professional wrestling must be giving its fans something genuine.

The fans of wrestling come to see skill, action, excitement. But it wasn't always that way. Fifty years ago a wrestling match meant two heavyweights locking each other up for an endless amount of time on the mat. People yawned. Then wrestling changed. The emphasis was shifted from defense to offense. Showmanship came in with flamboyant wrestlers like Gorgeous George. But the honesty and precision of the sport has never changed, except perhaps for the better. Professional wrestlers today are mostly college-educated men, many competed in the Olympics as amateurs, and they are definitely as fit as any other athletes.

Wrestling is a genuine sport as well as an entertainment, and its stars *are* genuine athletes. The long casualty lists of injured and maimed wrestlers provide unhappy evidence that what goes on in that ring is real and often dangerous competition.

There really has never been as much as a breath of scandal in this sport. The wrestlers and promoters are all honest citizens. Wrestlers show up for matches on time, do their work, and rarely complain. They are true professionals.

Which ultimately, I guess, brings us to this book. I am proud that it has finally come into being. I wrote it because I myself enjoy the tension and excitement, the display of skill and strength, that professional wrestling has to offer. As you can see, there are many pictures in it, for the electricity and excitement of a great match are primarily visual.

As for the written word, I have tried to profile the major stars, managers, matches, and events in professional wrestling. Of course, many will be missing, since there are hundreds of great wrestlers all over the country, and there aren't enough pages to accommodate all of them. But the legends, like Sammartino, Graham, Race, Gagne, Backlund, and Gorilla Monsoon, are all here in exclusive interviews.

Bob Backlund prepares Baron Mikel Scicluna for an atomic kneedrop. (*Frank Amato*)

INTRODUCTION

Jack Brisco tries to prevent Terry Funk from grabbing the ropes. (*Frank Amato*)

The scientific wrestlers and the rule-breakers are here. The clean fights and the terrible disasters. The mayhem and the contests of will and strength. The whole field is exciting—it is a sport that is never dull.

This is a fan's book, for the fans. I can tell you that from being around the arenas and the sportsmen as much as I have, I can offer nothing but praise and admiration to the people who keep thrilling the crowds and perpetuating the great tradition of pro wrestling.

So here is the book. For the good of professional wrestling and for all the fans, who are so loyal. And to those of you who are newcomers, here is a chance to see wrestling, to know it, and perhaps even to grow to enjoy it as much as all its fans do.

—R.M.

MAIN EVENT

★ 1 ★

The First Arena

A History of Wrestling to the Present Time

Of all the sports in the world, wrestling is, without a doubt, the oldest. Before the first caveman lit his first fire, animals in the wild were wrestling. Lions taught their little cubs the ways of survival through grappling and grabbing. All creatures of the earth would learn wrestling in their infancy so that they might go out into the world better protected against their predators.

The early caveman taught his children a variety of holds to use in the event they were attacked by a wild animal. No doubt he learned these holds from the mammals, for wrestling seems to be natural to all animals. Some scientists claim that wrestling is instinctive.

During the thousands of years that passed since the early caveman, many games were invented in order to pass time or meet challenges. But wrestling remained the individualistic game that taught survival. Wrestling as a sport is quite natural to man. It requires no equipment and is an effective way of developing energy, strong muscles and good health. All that is required in wrestling is a worthy opponent, and that may be found anywhere.

The oldest record that exists on wrestling goes back over five thousand years. A slab with two bronze figures was discovered in Mesopotamia, near Baghdad. It showed two standing men with their hands on each other's hips—two wrestlers engaged in combat. This find was made by Dr. S. A. Speiser of the University of Pennsylvania in 1938, but it symbolizes a culture that predates written history.

The Greek and Roman Periods

All through Greek and Roman history, wrestling played a prominent role. It was an honored sport, and many records of its importance in ancient culture still remain. The Greek ideal emphasized individual excellence and competition in all aspects of living—in sports and games as much as in philosophy, politics, or the arts.

The Greeks held wrestling in especially high esteem, second only to the discus, as a competitive sport. In the earliest Greek arenas, the rules for wrestling were pretty

3

Sandor Szabo (*left*) vs. Gorgeous George (*Courtesy of Global Wrestling Library*)

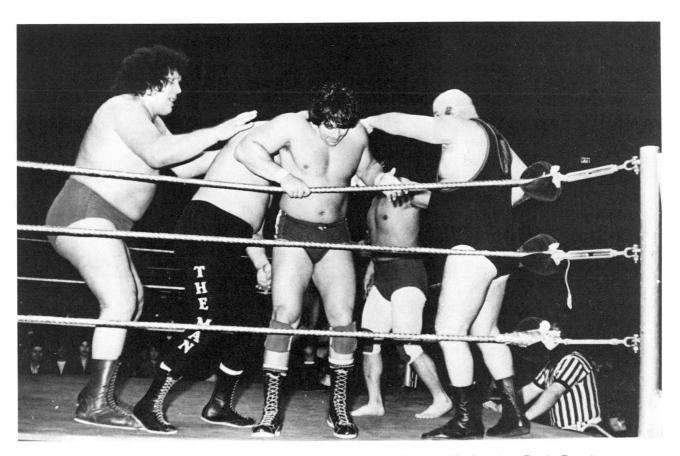

(*From left to right*) Andre the Giant, Stan Stasiak, Dino Bravo, and Butcher Vachon in a Battle Royal
(*George Napolitano*)

Rocky Johnson (*left*) vs. Jack Brisco (*Frank Amato*)

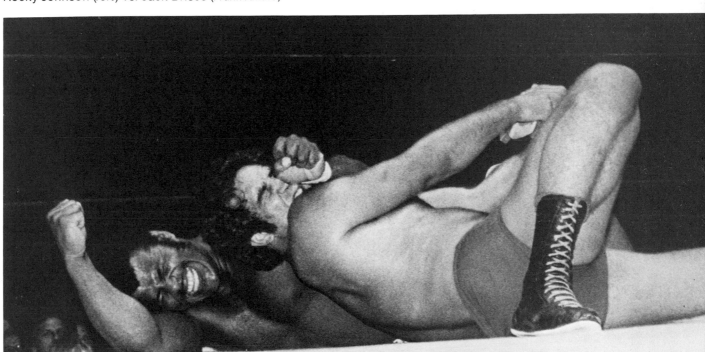

much the same as they are today in professional wrestling—with the important exception being that shaking one's opponent, eye-gouging and breaking fingers were permitted.

This developed into what was known as the *pancration,* a no-holds-barred style that was always rough and usually gory. Wrestlers could kick, punch, gouge, bite, strangle; they could do literally anything they wanted to win. The style went on in Greece until about 900 B.C., when Theseus, legendary king of Athens, decided to set down more stringent rules.

Baron von Raschke aims for the head of Bruno Sammartino. (*Frank Amato*)

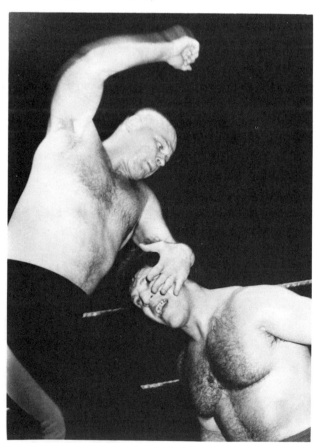

These new rules remained with the Greeks until the Roman conquest. Because the Romans had their own style of grappling, they combined their rules with Greek rules and Greco-Roman wrestling was born. The rules for Greco-Roman wrestling remain with us today in amateur and Olympic competition. In this form, holds are not permitted below the waist.

The most famous ancient Greek wrestler was Milo of Croton, who won six times at the Olympic and Isthmian games. Greek wrestlers often oiled their bodies before a match, the reason they gave being that it had some religious significance. The oil, of course, as we all know, prevents the opponent from getting any kind of hold applied and maintaining it. The Greeks also sprinkled "lucky dust" around the ring to appease the gods.

Music was almost always played at these festive events while the wrestling matches were going on. This custom was revived only once in the twentieth century, on January 21, 1944, when the Houston Symphony Orchestra played on the same bill with Lou Thesz and Wild Bill Longson, and King Kong Kox and Jack Kennedy. The orchestra actually accompanied one wrestling match on that card—between Ellis Bashara and Dave Levin. After the bout was over, Ellis Bashara, unwilling to have the concert come to an end too soon, walked, still bleeding, over to the podium, took the baton away from the conductor, and began to lead the orchestra himself!

After the Romans conquered Greece, they introduced a modified version of the Greek style, partly based on their own traditional rules, known as the Greco-Roman. This style was still much rougher and freer than the modern Greco-Roman style, which is practiced in many European countries and in the

Superstar Billy Graham with a headlock on Chief Jay
Strongbow (*Frank Amato*)

The Sport of Kings

Through the next thousand years after the twilight of Greece and Rome, a period known as the Dark Ages, history is mute on many things. But we do discover that wrestling became a local sport in this time as towns grew up in England and the rest of Europe. Nations at this point were struggling with other nations to expand their territories. Once the settlement of reasonable boundaries between countries was more or less established, wrestling again began to thrive on a national scale.

No longer were the Olympic games the center of international sports—the discus, the Marathon run, the jumping and running events were lost to history temporarily. Wrestling now emerged as the sport of kings, and became prominent all over the European continent and the British Isles.

Countries vied to produce the greatest champions. Royal titles, land, money, and armies were bet on the outcome of a single match. Prizes were awarded to the biggest, the strongest, the best wrestlers. Many of the monarchs of Europe held festivals and special feast days primarily to show off their champion wrestlers.

The competition during this period became as fierce as any war. Matches would be set up months in advance and each king would cheer on his champion to win for the honor of his country. No one knows what the king did to the loser, but we do know that the winner was praised and celebrated throughout the land, received prizes, and attended many feasts as the honored guest. This reveling and partying might go on and on until it was time for the champion to go off and conquer some new opponent from another nation.

Olympics today. This is a much slower-moving sport than professional wrestling because of the many rules that must be strictly adhered to. For example, no holds are permitted below the waist. Pro wrestling moves much faster; many wrestlers today complain that the more rules you make in pro wrestling, the slower the sport will become. To illustrate this point, take the case of the bout between Sweden's Algren and Finland's Bohling which took place at the 1912 Olympics in Stockholm. These two wrestlers fought for over six hours without a fall. The match, after all that time, ended without a decision!

Pete Sanchez (*left*) vs. Ric Flair (*Frank Amato*)

Killer Krupp attacks Bruiser Brody outside the ring. (*George Napolitano*)

Ivan Putski in control over Spiros Arion (*Frank Amato*)

THE FIRST ARENA

One of the most famous wrestling matches in history occurred in the early sixteenth century, though it didn't exactly take place in the ring. The opponents were King Francis I of France and King Henry VIII of England. It all started because the French wrestlers of that time were always defeated by the English, who seemed to produce the best wrestlers in that part of the world. Henry VIII, never one to keep silent, was always boasting about his wrestlers and made sure everyone in Europe knew about it. Well, Francis finally found a challenger who looked like he might be able to defeat the English champion. He sent the challenge to Henry and the match was set.

Henry and Francis shared the Royal Box for that day's bout. Henry began praising his wrestler rather loudly, shouting about the superior physical and mental abilities of the English. He went on to comment on how puny and inferior all Frenchmen were (using King Francis himself as an example).

Francis became infuriated, leapt from his seat, and grappled with Henry, trying to force him down for a pin. The bout did not last long and was called a draw, since the two monarchs' retinues rushed in to break it up.

During the sixteenth and seventeenth centuries England became the center of wrestling in Europe. There were almost as many different styles as there were English counties, and the most famous of these styles, the Cornish, the Devonshire, and the Lancashire, were named for their counties of origin. Each year on St. James's Day wrestlers from all over England, Scotland, and Ireland would gather in London for the national elimination matches.

The Scots and Irish always competed, but the sophisticated style of the English consistently proved too much for them. After several years of being defeated by English wrestlers, Scottish and Irish grapplers decided to form their own methods. The Irish developed a style that was more rough-and-tumble and more brutal than the English; the Scottish was similar to the Lancashire style, but with tricky variations.

The French, who were still wrestling, though they no longer challenged the supremacy of the English, also evolved a national style which became the basis of modern Greco-Roman wrestling. The Germans also wrestled avidly, but their bouts were generally confined to the mat or the ground. Whatever the style, the sport flourished in Europe, as it continues to do today.

American wrestling, of course, was derived from the several British styles. But in such a melting-pot of nationalities, other styles from Europe, Asia, and Africa were inevitably blended into it.

George "the Animal" Steele (*left*) vs. Bruno Sammartino (*George Napolitano*)

Andre the Giant vs. Antonio Inoki (*Koichi*)

Out of the Orient

It was several years into the twentieth century before Oriental wrestling became known in the United States, but it had already existed for a long, long time before that. Nowhere in Asia is wrestling more popular than in Japan, where it has been the national sport for at least 2000 years. The Japanese emperors, just as the kings of Europe did, greatly enjoyed wrestling contests and established festival days in which they could highlight the bouts. The favored wrestler of the emperor was called the *sumo,* and sumo wrestling has always been a greatly honored profession in Japan. So important was the masterful and large physique of a sumo wrestler that these men of immensely broad proportions have been in-termarrying with the daughters of other sumo wrestlers for over 20 centuries. Long before western man discovered the principle of interbreeding, the sumo wrestlers were using this technique to develop generations of men with these powerful bodies. The average sumo wrestler stands about 5 feet 8 inches (which is tall by Japanese standards) and weighs between 300 and 400 pounds!

Out of the Japanese style of wrestling came ju jitsu, from which was born judo—two of the more popular martial arts, both known and respected worldwide. It is also interesting to note that for many hundreds of years wrestling has been taught to Japanese soldiers as part of their military training, and as a result the Japanese soldier is feared for his awesome skill at hand-to-hand combat.

Cowboys, Indians, and Pioneers

American Indians have many legends about wrestling and it is a highly honorable activity in many of their cultures. Though the form of wrestling you see today is not directly related to any particular Indian style, many holds were developed from Indian techniques of hand-to-hand combat against the invading palefaces.

In the eighteenth and nineteenth centuries in America, most of the wrestling done was of the Greco-Roman style. The style of wrestling that emerged on the newly settled frontier was called catch-as-catch-can (or free-style) wrestling, which meant that you could do whatever you had to do to win.

This exhibition wrestling was generally presented for a small admission charge on the stage of a dance hall or in a saloon. For part of the eighteenth century wrestling was a sport enjoyed by the fragile ladies of the day as much as by their men.

Exhibitions of Greco-Roman wrestling were still put on for small groups in taverns and carnival sideshows until the end of the nineteenth century. Then a new development occurred. Carnivals began to offer cash prizes to any local citizens who could pin the carnival's champ. During this period, when boasting was rampant, most men thought that they could wrestle. They believed that all you needed was a muscular body and some degree of strength. People remembered that Abraham Lincoln wrestled in his youth, so they thought, "Why not? If the President can wrestle, so can I!"

These local boasters would step into the ring with the champ, a strong man who had been wrestling for ten or fifteen years. Once in the ring, they would strip down to their red longjohns and be instructed briefly in some of the rules of Greco-Roman wrestling. Needless to say, the majority of these local challengers did not win. To be kind, one might say they always came in second.

During Abe Lincoln's time, free-style wrestling became very popular in America, and catch-as-catch-can was on the rise again. The Americans at this time more or less abandoned the Greco-Roman form and used this free-style instead because the crowds insisted it was more interesting to watch.

The New Style Takes Hold

The first American professional wrestler to advocate free-style competition was Tom Jenkins. He came from Cleveland, Ohio, where he had been a worker in a rolling mill.

Tom Jenkins had only one good eye. He used any hold or maneuver he could to win, and he soon became something of a folk hero.

But Jenkins never counted on Frank Gotch. When Gotch approached him for a bout, he was slightly amused, because Gotch was a much smaller and lighter man than Jenkins. Tom saw him as one of the easiest opponents he had ever had to face. "Frank Gotch," the fans insisted, "will lose to the mighty man of Cleveland."

What the fans and Jenkins didn't know was that Gotch, though small and light, was extremely powerful. He was also a master of all holds; he was daring, fast and highly intelligent. Tom Jenkins was a powerful man who didn't know much about leverage. Unfortunately for him, Frank Gotch knew a great deal about leverage. So in 1904, Jenkins learned from Gotch that there was more to wrestling than just brute strength, when the smaller man easily took the championship away from him.

Many wrestlers of the Greco-Roman school tried unsuccessfully to defeat Gotch, even when they resorted to using a freer style. Gotch held his title until 1913, losing it only once for a very short time to Freddie Beall, when Beall knocked Frank's head against the ringpost and Gotch passed out. Though Beall made the pin, the rematch found Gotch quite awake and toying with Beall before he set in for the kill and regained that championship with supreme ease.

In the years he was champ, Gotch fought 160 matches and won 154 of them. By modern professional wrestling standards 160 bouts is less than a year's work for a grappler!

Frank Gotch retired in 1913 with the title of undefeated Heavyweight Champion.

Wrestling Becomes Organized

After Frank Gotch won the title from Tom Jenkins in 1904, a number of promoters around at that time felt it was necessary to form an alliance of some kind. There were many wrestlers and many nonwrestlers around laying claim to the title of World Heavyweight Champion. In order to establish this championship it became necessary to form such an alliance in order to insure the title to one person and allow this titleholder to take on any challenges that might come up. Frank Gotch, the first titleholder recognized in the United States, gained his title not from his bout with Tom Jenkins, but in a later one with George Hackenschmidt, the man who claimed he was the World Heavyweight Champion. Their battle was also fought in 1905, and Gotch was again the winner, this time over a man many considered to be the greatest wrestler in the world.

Many fans speculate on who *is* the greatest wrestler of all time, but offering only one name would not be enough to answer such a question. Some believe it was Frank Gotch, because of his ability to get out of holds and get his opponents into unbreakable ones; some say George Hackenschmidt, the Russian Lion, who was one of the greatest scientific wrestlers. He was a powerful man and a perfectionist, disliking rough or dirty tactics. He stood 5 feet 10 inches, weighed between 208 and 225 pounds, and had a reach of 75 inches. Still, he wrestled Gotch in 1905 and in 1908 and lost both times, and again in 1911—and lost.

Other great names which appeared later in wrestling history include Gama the Great, from India; Youseff Mahmout, the original Terrible Turk; Strangler Lewis; Stanislaus Zbyszko; Dick Shikat; Jim Londos; Jim Browning; Ray Steele; and Rudy Dusek, who all fought in the 1930s. In the '40s and '50s there was Lou Thesz, Edouard Carpentier, Whippier Billy Watson, Bill Longson, and Bobby Managoff. In the '60s and '70s one thinks of Buddy Rogers, Gene Kiniski, Dory Funk, Jr., Harley Race, Verne Gagne, Jack Brisco, Bruno Sammartino, and countless others.

Heavyweight wrestling gained tremendously in popularity at the end of World War II. The men were back from battle, the economy was booming, and people had more time for leisure activities. Interest in the masters of the mat picked up all over the

The legendary champion, Lou Thesz (*Courtesy of Global Wrestling Library*)

country. There were more and more wrestlers appearing on the scene every day, and more and more wrestling promoters. The men who made the matches were starting to have difficulty in planning enough of them to keep the growing number of fans happy.

Wrestling was now a nationwide sport, no longer confined to large cities. More people owned cars and were more than willing to drive many miles to see a good grappling card. Smaller towns began to book wrestling events.

Professional wrestling did add one important element to its appeal in the 1940s and 1950s, in the person of George Wagner. George was an expert, tough, and very ordinary wrestler. But when he decided to set his hair and dye it blond, hire a "valet" to spray perfume and incense around the ring (remember the Greeks who scattered "lucky dust" in ancient times?), and refuse to be touched by anyone—he became Gorgeous George. He was still an expert wrestler, still tough, but no longer ordinary. He became a number-one box office attraction. Since Wagner (who died in 1963 at age 48), a number of other wrestlers have found that they can increase their appeal to the crowd by enhancing their personalities in the way that Gorgeous George did.

The National Wrestling Alliance (NWA)

In 1948 five wrestling promoters got together to form a stronger wrestling association, which later came to be known as the National Wrestling Alliance (NWA). Of that original group, Sam Munchnick is still promoting bouts in the St. Louis area. The origi-

Harley Race over Rocky Johnson (*Frank Amato*)

Ric Flair with the edge on Pete Sanchez (*Frank Amato*)

New Zealand, with affiliates in Asia and Europe. It is a solid organization which contributes a great deal of money to charitable causes, as well as to the United States Olympic Wrestling Team. Another of their philanthropic activities is an educational campaign designed to warn young people about the dangers of drug abuse.

The presidents of the NWA have been Sam Munchnick (who held that office the longest—for 22 years), Pinky George, Frank Tunney, Fred Kohler, Karl Sarpolis, and Jack Adkisson. The current president is Bob Geigel.

The American Wrestling Association (AWA)

The question of who holds the title always seems to be at the heart of any controversy in organized wrestling. On June 14, 1957, there was a title bout held in Chicago between Edouard Carpentier and Lou Thesz. Carpentier defeated Thesz, but Thesz, by virtue of certain rules, still held the title and the world heavyweight belt.

However, a group of promoters who were dissatisfied with this decision recognized Carpentier as the new champion and organized a series of bouts for him under that billing. In 1958 Carpentier was defeated by Verne Gagne, who subsequently lost and then regained the belt. In 1960 Gagne challenged the current NWA champion, Pat O'Connor, to a title bout. O'Connor did not respond and thus on August 16, 1960, Gagne was declared the first American Wrestling Association Champion. The AWA was now formed, and its championship belt has changed hands more than 35 times in the last 20 years.

There was a movement started in 1977,

nal purpose of the NWA was, first, to reestablish the disputed world championship title, once and for all this time, and, second, to parcel out limited territories to the more than 500 wrestling promoters in the United States and Canada. The trouble was that some promoters were lining up bouts in other promoters' territories, a form of unfair competition with other promoters who were then not able to get wrestlers in their own areas. This led to many disputes among the promoters themselves, as well as a lot of confusion for the fans. The NWA arranged for the best wrestlers to be exchanged among the different areas, which guaranteed a wider audience for the stars and some of the newcomers in this country and overseas.

The NWA represents promoters in the United States, Canada, Japan, Australia, and

headed by Paul Boesch of Houston, Texas, to reunite the NWA and the AWA. This gave rise to a card that was held on October 21, 1977, in Houston, that featured NWA champion Harley Race against Ox Baker and AWA champion Nick Bockwinkle against Terry Funk.

It might appear on the surface that there is animosity between wrestling organizations;

however, there is not. Promoters from one association are quite friendly with promoters from another, and they get along well in their professional and social lives. Many wrestlers cross boundaries and are welcome in arenas all over the country, and overseas as well. Wrestlers are not tied down to any one association; they are free agents and may contract to fight more or less wherever they please. They usually end up fighting in one area, but only because of the prohibitive amount of traveling they would otherwise be subject to.

It is important to mention this in order to stress that the split between the NWA and the AWA did not in any way detract from the great sport of professional wrestling; rather, it enhanced it, creating a more vigorous and competitive atmosphere in which promoters are all intent on bringing the best possible bouts to the fans.

Verne Gagne with son Greg (*George Napolitano*)

The World Wide Wrestling Federation (WWWF)

Alas, still another controversy was to arise over the heavyweight wrestling championship, and again we find Lou Thesz right in the middle of it. On January 24, 1963, in Toronto, Canada, Thesz, the contender, defeated NWA champion Buddy Rogers in one fall. A rematch was held two weeks later, and Thesz once again defeated Rogers in one fall. Many of the East Coast promoters contested this decision, insisting that a championship match could not be judged on the basis of a single fall.

These East Coast promoters formed their own organization, which they called the World Wide Wrestling Federation (WWWF),

Opposite: Ray Stevens executes his "bombs away" maneuver on El Olympico. (*George Napolitano*)

The handshake of championship—Bruno Sammartino (*left*) and Bob Backlund (*Frank Amato*)

and proclaimed Buddy Rogers as their first champion.

A few months later, on May 17, 1963, Rogers was rather at ease when he stepped into the ring with an Italian strongman named Bruno Sammartino. After all, Buddy was the champ. He had defeated Bruno before and there was no reason why he couldn't do it again. However, that was not the way it turned out. Wrestling history was made in 47 seconds as Sammartino grabbed Rogers, threw him into the ropes, caught him on the rebound, enfolded him in his famous bearhug, lifted him high in the air,

then applied a backbreaker, and Buddy Rogers relinquished the championship.

Bruno Sammartino held the title for seven years and seven months, meeting all challengers and defeating every one of them. Then, on the night of January 18, 1971, he met Ivan Koloff in Madison Square Garden. They fought for what seemed like an eternity; Bruno Sammartino, the Living Legend, and Ivan Koloff, the Russian Bear, ready to do anything to win the belt. Exhausted, both wrestlers went down to the mat. It seemed as if they both had their shoulders pinned. The referee counted, one . . . two . . . three!

Who had won? "The new World Wide Wrestling Federation Champion, Ivan Koloff," said the ring announcer. The fans were stunned. They looked at Bruno, who was also stunned. They looked at Koloff, the new champion. He was stunned. The title had finally changed hands after seven years, seven months, and one day.

Ivan Koloff was not to taste victory for long. One month later, again in Madison Square Garden, Ivan Koloff met Pedro Morales. Koloff went down to defeat in 10 minutes and 40 seconds.

Pedro Morales held the WWWF heavyweight belt for more than two years. During this time he fought a classic scientific match with Bruno Sammartino which ended in a draw after more than an hour. After the match was over, the two embraced in mutual admiration.

In Philadelphia, on December 1, 1973, Morales encountered Stan "the Man" Stasiak in the squared circle. Stan heartpunched his way to victory and became the new champion for a very short time—nine days, to be exact. On December 10, 1973, Stasiak found himself facing the Living

THE FIRST ARENA

Legend, Bruno Sammartino, in Madison Square Garden.

Bruno's agility, skill, experience, and, of course, strength, withstood Stasiak's bru- tal "heartpunch" and the belt once again belonged to Sammartino. Never before, or since, has anyone won the WWWF belt twice.

Bruno Sammartino locks onto Bobby Duncum (*Frank Amato*)

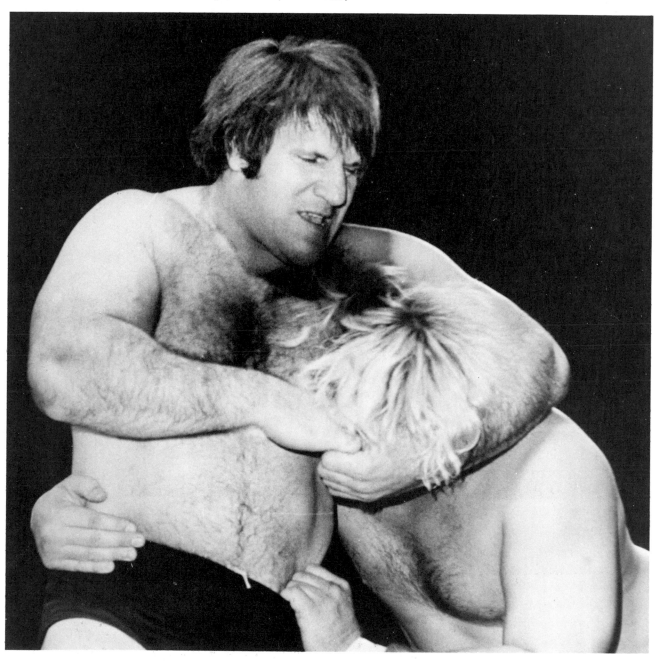

Superstar Billy Graham with an edge over Bob Backlund in the Steel Cage (*Frank Amato*)

Bruno Sammartino's second reign of three and a half years came to an end when he met Superstar Billy Graham at the Baltimore Civic Center on the night of April 30, 1977. The year before, Sammartino had actually had his neck broken in a bout with Stan Hansen in Madison Square Garden. Although his doctors predicted that he would be forced to retire from wrestling, Bruno returned to face Hansen just two months later and defeated him with ease.

Bruno had faced Superstar Billy Graham before, but this crucial contest was not going to be so easy. Graham was credited with the pin, but many witnesses at ringside claimed he used the ropes for leverage—which, of course, is illegal. Nevertheless, Superstar took the belt away and held it for about ten months.

Graham had also faced many tough oppo-nents and so he wasn't particularly wary when young Bob Backlund stepped into the Garden ring with him on the night of February 20, 1978. Backlund defeated Superstar, although this match was also disputed, since Graham's foot was allegedly over the top rope when Backlund made the pin. Backlund agreed to a rematch. This time Graham won by a decision—Backlund was bleeding so badly that the match had to be stopped. There was no pin, and Superstar did not get his belt back.

This rivalry was finally settled by a famous Steel-Cage Match. After a period of action-packed fighting, the Superstar got his leg caught in the bars of the cage, and Bob Backlund climbed out of the cage, announcing to the wrestling world that he was the World Wide Wrestling Federation Heavyweight Champion.

The Future

The National Wrestling Alliance Heavyweight Championship changed hands 41 times since Frank Gotch's victory over George Hackenschmidt; the AWA belt, 35 times; the WWWF belt, 7 times. From the days of the Greeks that belt has changed hands more times than we could ever count. But the champions and the contenders are not forgotten; they live on in the history of a great sporting tradition.

From a tactic of survival to an occasion for celebration, to the sport of kings and emperors, to the main event in arenas sold out each and every night all over the country, wrestling has never weakened or faded in appeal. It is a sport that audiences in all times, in all countries, have enjoyed. It is the oldest sport, and yet because of the excitement it generates, it always seems new.

What can we look for in the future? More great champions, more skillful battles, and more and more fans to fill the arenas—the action and excitement of professional wrestling.

An Explanation of the Various Championship Belts

Over the past 75 years there have been many titles, titleholders, and claimants to those titles. Many of today's wrestling associations were originally formed to determine the rightful owners of those belts. Today anyone holding a title has fought the contenders in his area and has a right to wear that championship belt.

On the North American continent there are several titleholders who are considered to be world championship caliber. These men wear their belts by virtue of the fact that they have defeated all contenders in their area. If a contender for the belt from another area wants to win the title all he has to do is defeat the current champion.

The three major world heavyweight titles are sanctioned by the three largest wrestling associations: the American Wrestling Association (AWA), the National Wrestling Alliance (NWA), and the World Wide Wrestling Federation (WWWF). The NWA World Heavyweight Championship, which was first awarded to Frank Gotch in 1904, is the oldest belt recognized in the United States.

In addition to these three major belts, there are a number of other belts, which are regional. The United States Heavyweight Championship is a title currently recognized in three areas of the United States—the Mid-Atlantic region, the Michigan region, and Northern California. There are three titleholders today who possess that belt.

The oldest American title, the United States Belt, started in San Francisco in the 1950s, when the *Police Gazette* awarded it to Verne Gagne. The North American Heavyweight Championship is another regional title, which can be defended anywhere on the North American continent.

There are also smaller regional belts which are limited to states or particular areas of the country. The Mid-Atlantic Belt is one of these. Other state or area belts include those awarded by California, Georgia, Florida, Hawaii (called the Ring Belt and started right after World War II, when Hawaii was still a territory), Missouri, New England, the Pacific Coast, the Rocky Mountain region, the Southern region, Southwestern region, Texas, and Vermont (which claims the oldest belt in history, dating back to 1860).

There are also province championships in

Canada. Among these are the British Columbia Belt, the Maritime Provinces Belt, and the Quebec Belt.

Although they are not too popular today, city titles are also awarded. Two of these were the New York City Championship, given back in the 1950s, and the Santa Monica Belt, which was won by top California wrestlers.

For tag team competition the major belts recognized in the United States are those sanctioned by the American Wrestling Association, the World Wrestling Association in Indianapolis, and the World Wide Wrestling Federation. There are also tag team belts recognized in various regions, but they are not sanctioned by the National Wrestling Alliance, which governs wrestling in these areas. They include titles awarded in Georgia, the Mid-Atlantic states, the Pacific Northwest, and Vancouver, British Columbia.

National Wrestling Alliance Titles

DATE	WINNER	OPPONENT DEFEATED	LOCATION
1895	MARTIN (FARMER) BURNS	Evan (Strangler) Lewis	
1897	TOM JENKINS	Martin (Farmer) Burns	Cleveland
1902	DAN MC LEOD	Tom Jenkins	
1903	TOM JENKINS	Dan Mc Leod	Worcester
1904	FRANK GOTCH	Tom Jenkins	Bellingham
1905	TOM JENKINS	Frank Gotch	New York
1905	GEORGE HACKENSCHMIDT	Tom Jenkins	New York
1905	FRANK GOTCH [1]	George Hackenschmidt	Chicago
1906	FRED BEALL	Frank Gotch	New Orleans
1906	FRANK GOTCH	Fred Beall	
1913	FRANK GOTCH (Retired)		
1913	HENRY ORDEMAN	Jess Westegard	Omaha
1914	CHARLEY CUTLER	Henry Ordeman	Minneapolis
1915	JOE STECHER	Charley Cutler	Omaha
1917	EARL CADDOCK	Joe Stecher	Omaha
1920	JOE STECHER	Earl Caddock	New York
1920	ED (STRANGLER) LEWIS	Joe Stecher	New York
1922	STANISLAUS ZBYSZKO	Ed (Strangler) Lewis	New York
1922	ED (STRANGLER) LEWIS	Stanislaus Zbyszko	Wichita
1925	WAYNE MUNN	Ed (Strangler) Lewis	Kansas City
1925	STANISLAUS ZBYSZKO	Wayne Munn	Philadelphia
1925	JOE STECHER	Stanislaus Zbyszko	St. Louis
1928	ED (STRANGLER) LEWIS	Joe Stecher	St. Louis
1929	GUS SONNENBERG	Ed (Strangler) Lewis	Boston
1931	ED DON GEORGE	Gus Sonnenberg	Boston
1931	ED (STRANGLER) LEWIS	Ed Don George	Los Angeles
1931	HENRY DE GLANE	Ed (Strangler) Lewis	Montreal
1931	ED DON GEORGE	Henry De Glane	Boston

[1] First recognized NWA champion.

National Wrestling Alliance Titles

DATE	WINNER	OPPONENT DEFEATED	LOCATION
1929	DICK SHIKAT	Jim Londos [1]	Philadelphia
Jun. 6, 1930	JIM LONDOS	Dick Shikat	Philadelphia
1932	ED (STRANGLER) LEWIS	Dick Shikat	Long Island City
1933	JIM BROWNING	Ed (Strangler) Lewis	New York
1934	JIM LONDOS	Jim Browning	New York
Jun. 27, 1935	DANNO O'MAHONEY	Jim Londos	Boston
Jun. 30, 1935	DANNO O'MAHONEY	Ed Don George	Boston
1936	DICK SHIKAT	Danno O'Mahoney	New York
1936	ALI BABA	Dick Shikat	Detroit
Jun. 26, 1936	EVERETT MARSHALL	Ali Baba	Columbus
Dec. 29, 1937	LOU THESZ	Everett Marshall [2]	St. Louis
Feb. 11, 1938	STEVE (CRUSHER) CASEY	Lou Thesz	Boston
Feb. 23, 1939	LOU THESZ	Everett Marshall	St. Louis
Jun. 23, 1939	BRONKO NAGURSKI	Lou Thesz	Houston
Mar. 7, 1940	RAY STEELE	Bronko Nagurski	St. Louis
Mar. 11, 1941	BRONKO NAGURSKI	Ray Steele	Minneapolis
Jun. 5, 1941	SANDOR SZABO	Bronko Nagurski	St. Louis
Feb. 19, 1942	BILL LONGSON	Sandor Szabo	St. Louis
Oct. 7, 1942	YVON ROBERT	Bill Longson	Montreal
Nov. 27, 1942	BOBBY MANAGOFF	Yvon Robert	Houston
Feb. 19, 1943	BILL LONGSON	Bobby Managoff	St. Louis
Feb. 21, 1947	WHIPPER BILLY WATSON	Bill Longson	St. Louis
Apr. 25, 1947	LOU THESZ	Whipper Billy Watson	St. Louis
Nov. 21, 1947	BILL LONGSON	Lou Thesz	St. Louis
Jul. 20, 1948	LOU THESZ	Bill Longson	Indianapolis

National Wrestling Alliance Titles

DATE	WINNER	OPPONENT DEFEATED	LOCATION
Mar. 15, 1956	WHIPPER BILLY WATSON	Lou Thesz	Toronto
Nov. 9, 1956	LOU THESZ	Whipper Billy Watson	St. Louis
Nov. 14, 1957	DICK HUTTON	Lou Thesz	Toronto
Jan. 9, 1959	PAT O'CONNOR	Dick Hutton	St. Louis
Jun. 30, 1961	BUDDY ROGERS	Pat O'Connor	Chicago
Jan. 24, 1963	LOU THESZ	Buddy Rogers	Toronto
Jan. 7, 1966	GENE KINISKI	Lou Thesz	St. Louis
Feb. 11, 1969	DORY FUNK, JR.	Gene Kiniski	Tampa

[1] In 1929 Jim Londos had claimed the world heavyweight title, in spite of the fact that there were other titleholders at that time. In 1934 Londos challenged the current titleholder, Jim Browning, and defeated him, thus establishing legitimate claim to the title.

[2] In 1938 the NWA recognized Everett Marshall as the titleholder, since the last winner of the belt, Steve Casey, was out of the country and would not defend his title.

National Wrestling Alliance Titles (cont.)

DATE	WINNER	OPPONENT DEFEATED	LOCATION
May 24, 1973	HARLEY RACE	Dory Funk, Jr.	Kansas City
Jul. 20, 1973	JACK BRISCO	Harley Race	Houston
Dec. 2, 1974	SHOHEI "GIANT" BABA	Jack Brisco	Kagoshimi
Dec. 9, 1974	JACK BRISCO	Shohei "Giant" Baba	Tokyo
Dec. 10, 1975	TERRY FUNK	Jack Brisco	Miami Beach
Feb. 6, 1977	HARLEY RACE	Terry Funk	Toronto

American Wrestling Association Titles

DATE	WINNER	OPPONENT DEFEATED	LOCATION
Jun. 14, 1957	EDOUARD CARPENTIER	Lou Thesz	Chicago
Aug. 1958	VERNE GAGNE	Edouard Carpentier	Omaha
Nov. 1958	WILBUR SNYDER	Verne Gagne	Omaha
Aug. 1959	DOCTOR X	Wilbur Snyder	Omaha[1]
Feb. 26, 1960	VERNE GAGNE	Doctor X[2]	Omaha
Jul. 11, 1961	GENE KINISKI	Verne Gagne	Minneapolis
Aug. 8, 1961	VERNE GAGNE	Gene Kiniski	Minneapolis
Jan. 9, 1962	MISTER M	Verne Gagne	Minneapolis
Aug. 21, 1962	VERNE GAGNE	Mister M	Minneapolis
Jul. 9, 1963	CRUSHER LISOWSKI	Verne Gagne	Minneapolis
Jul. 20, 1963	VERNE GAGNE	Crusher Lisowski	Minneapolis
Jul. 27, 1963	FRITZ VON ERICH	Verne Gagne	Omaha
Aug. 8, 1963	VERNE GAGNE	Fritz Von Erich	Amarillo
Nov. 28, 1963	THE CRUSHER	Verne Gagne	St. Paul
Dec. 14, 1963	VERNE GAGNE	The Crusher	Minneapolis
May 2, 1964	MAD DOG VACHON	Verne Gagne	Omaha
May 16, 1964	VERNE GAGNE	Mad Dog Vachon	Omaha
Oct. 20, 1964	MAD DOG VACHON	Verne Gagne	Minneapolis
May 15, 1965	IGOR VODIC	Mad Dog Vachon	Omaha
May 22, 1965	MAD DOG VACHON	Igor Vodic	Omaha
Aug. 21, 1965	THE CRUSHER	Mad Dog Vachon	St. Paul
Nov. 12, 1965	MAD DOG VACHON	The Crusher	Denver
Nov. 12, 1966	DICK THE BRUISER	Mad Dog Vachon	Omaha
Nov. 19, 1966	MAD DOG VACHON	Dick the Bruiser	Omaha

[1] From February 1960 until September 1963 there were two AWA heavyweight titles. One was known as the Minneapolis Title, the other as the Omaha Title.
[2] Doctor X (later known as Mister M) was Bill Miller.

American Wrestling Association Titles (cont.)

DATE	WINNER	OPPONENT DEFEATED	LOCATION
Feb. 26, 1967	VERNE GAGNE	Mad Dog Vachon	St. Paul
Aug. 17, 1968	DICK BEYERS [1]	Verne Gagne	Bloomington
Aug. 31, 1968	VERNE GAGNE	Dick Beyers	Minneapolis
Nov. 8, 1975	NICK BOCKWINKLE	Verne Gagne	St. Paul

American Wrestling Association Titles

DATE	WINNER	OPPONENT DEFEATED	LOCATION
Jun. 14, 1957	EDOUARD CARPENTIER [2]	Lou Thesz	Chicago
Aug. 1958	VERNE GAGNE	Edouard Carpentier	Omaha
Nov. 1958	WILBUR SNYDER	Verne Gagne	Omaha
Aug. 1959	DOCTOR X	Wilbur Snyder	Omaha
Feb. 1961	DON LEO JONATHAN	Doctor X	Omaha
Mar. 2, 1961	DOCTOR X	Don Leo Jonathan	Omaha
Apr. 7, 1961	DON LEO JONATHAN	Doctor X	Omaha
Sep. 16, 1961	VERNE GAGNE	Don Leo Jonathan	Omaha
Jul. 21, 1962	FRITZ VON ERICH	Verne Gagne	Omaha
Aug. 25, 1962	VERNE GAGNE	Fritz Von Erich	Omaha
Feb. 15, 1963	CRUSHER LISOWSKI	Verne Gagne	Omaha
Jul. 20, 1963	VERNE GAGNE	Crusher Lisowski	Minneapolis
Jul. 27, 1963	FRITZ VON ERICH	Verne Gagne	Omaha
Sep. 7, 1963	VERNE GAGNE	Fritz Von Erich	Omaha

World Wide Wrestling Federation Titles

DATE	WINNER	OPPONENT DEFEATED	LOCATION
Jan. 24, 1963	BUDDY ROGERS	Lou Thesz	Toronto
May 17, 1963	BRUNO SAMMARTINO	Buddy Rogers	New York
Jan. 18, 1971	IVAN KOLOFF	Bruno Sammartino	New York

[1] Dick Beyers, who defeated Verne Gagne on August 17, 1968, was also known as Doctor X.

[2] The following are the holders of the Omaha Title; the two titles were consolidated into a single AWA belt when Verne Gagne won both of them, on August 25 and on September 7, 1963.

World Wide Wrestling Federation Titles (cont.)

DATE	WINNER	OPPONENT DEFEATED	LOCATION
Feb. 8, 1971	PEDRO MORALES	Ivan Koloff	New York
Dec. 1, 1973	STAN STASIAK	Pedro Morales	Philadelphia
Dec. 9, 1973	BRUNO SAMMARTINO	Stan Stasiak	New York
Apr. 30, 1977	BILLY GRAHAM	Bruno Sammartino	Baltimore
Feb. 20, 1978	BOB BACKLUND	Billy Graham	New York

★ 2 ★

The Stars

The excitement and action of professional wrestling comes from only one source: the wrestlers. So naturally they are the most important part of any book on the sport. Their individual styles, techniques, and personalities are what intrigue the fans and make the sport such an entertaining one to watch.

There are wrestlers who are fine athletes and ethical men, who are scientifically excellent and who bring honor to the squared circle. And then there are those who fall under the heading of rulebreakers, wrestlers who use brutal, vicious tactics in the ring, who delight in hurting opponents, who will resort to any means, no matter how cruel, to win their match.

For this section I have selected what I believe to be the top stars today in professional wrestling: men on the mat who exhibit, for good or evil, an awesome combination of strength and stamina. Here are the rulebreakers and the scientific athletes, speaking their minds about what they do and how they do it. Of course, there will be some favorites that have been left out. But that must be expected, since the selection was purely subjective. Some who are not here are profiled later on in Chapter Six, which is more extensive.

I hope you will find that most of the stars profiled here are among *your* favorites, and that the portraits of their personalities, backgrounds, and goals are both interesting and enlightening.

Superstar Billy Graham (*bottom*) vs. Dusty Rhodes (*Frank Amato*)

Andre the Giant

"Well, I've been wrestling for over 12 years, and you can figure at least 5 matches a week. Sometimes I've had 7 matches a week. *And I've never lost a match.*"

This incredible statement is absolutely true. It comes from a man who has never been pinned on that mat to the count of three; a wrestler who has never lost a match. He is called the Eighth Wonder of the World. Standing 7 feet 4 inches and weighing in at 472 pounds, he is the unbelievable and undefeatable Andre the Giant.

Andre the Giant (*Frank Amato*)

If you were to mention quickly, off the top of your head, the most popular wrestlers today, you would probably name Bruno Sammartino, Dusty Rhodes, Rick Steamboat, and Verne Gagne—but right up there, probably near or at the top of the list, would be Andre the Giant. Any card that boasts his name assures a packed arena; when he walks into that ring, the roar of the crowd is staggering. His skill and strength combined with his stamina and amazing size make Andre a phenomenon in the ring; one can often see him tossing his 260-odd-pound opponents around as though they were rag dolls.

Yet, Andre has never worn a belt, even though he is undefeated. Many fans think this is unfair, but Andre sees it another way. "I've been asked to fight for the belt a few times," he tells me. "But first of all, if I was champion I couldn't go where I want, all over the world. I'm a big attraction right now. Therefore one attraction is the champion, and I'm an attraction too. Makes two instead of one for the people to see."

The Giant from the French Alps is not as popular as he is solely because of his size. There are other super-large wrestlers (though not quite as large as Andre), like Ernie Ladd, Don Leo Jonathan, and Shohei Baba, but Andre seems to have the greatest appeal of them all. For one thing, he is a decent man, a respected athlete, who rarely breaks the rules unless provoked to defend himself. Another thing that captivates the fans is his strength, which is awesome. Only Don Leo Jonathan and Killer Kowalski have ever been able to lift him off the mat. And no

Andre the Giant vs. Ernie Ladd (*George Napolitano*)

one has ever gotten Andre over the top rope.

"I'm in Battle Royals with 18 or 20 wrestlers," he says with a smile. "Of course they want to get me out of there. But they have never gotten me over the top rope yet. They're still trying."

Andre comes off the farm in Mollien, France. When he was in his teens, he had already reached seven feet in height. He became involved in sports when he came to Paris. "I used to play soccer and rugby and come to all the matches in Paris, and I asked

Andre the Giant vs. Ernie Ladd (*George Napolitano*)

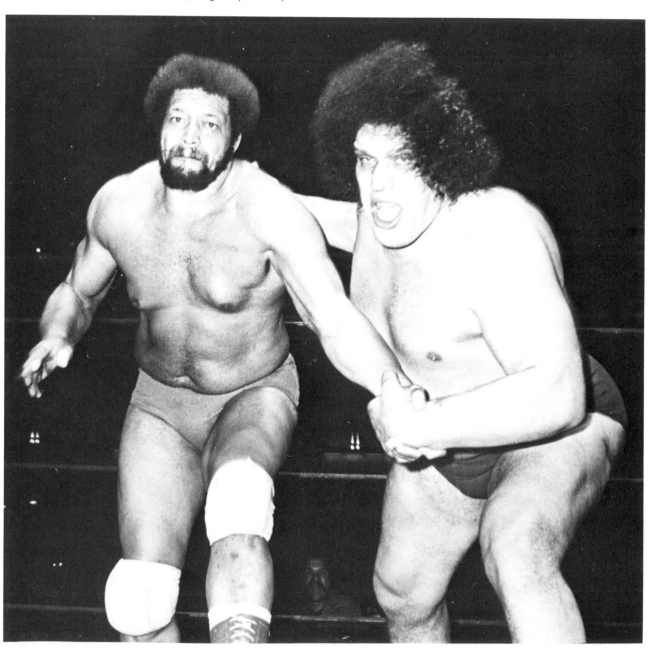

how I could get into wrestling. When I went down to the gym, people involved with wrestling saw that I was in good condition and all I needed was to learn the skills. Six months after that they set up the first match for me."

Edouard Carpentier, the Flying Frenchman, a legendary mat hero, took a keen interest in the Giant and put him through rigorous training, and not long after Andre was winning bout after bout in France. Soon he was being matched against two and even three wrestlers at a time. Andre still won easily.

Andre's next move was to Canada, then to the AWA, and as always he proved his wrestling skills and became a fan favorite. He then moved to the WWWF region and completely won the loyalty of the crowds. He faced such opponents as Professor Tanaka, Stan Stasiak, Larry Hennig, Blackjack Lanza, and Buddy Wolf, and of course won all his matches. His regular tag team partners became Chief Jay Strongbow and Pedro Morales.

Matchmakers from all over the world now wanted Andre on their cards. Regularly Andre would wrestle one night in New York, the following night in Texas, and the next night in California. Japan was also a frequent stop.

The fans were always behind him, growing in numbers and devotion. And this has meant a lot to Andre over the years. "I love to be around people," he says. "I love every-body." Clearly the affection works both ways.

Though Andre has never been pinned, he has been knocked down. In the beginning of his career it happened more frequently than it does now. "Some guys had 25 or 30 years experience. Now I have the experience, the size, and the speed." This all goes to explain why Andre has never lost a match in 12 years.

He is well liked among wrestlers and has his own favorites in the ring, among them Bruno Sammartino, Bobby Backlund, Peter Maivia, and Superstar Graham. "They're all top wrestlers," he affirms.

Unlike his peers, Andre does not spend hours each day at the gym. In fact, he rarely trains, being as fit as he is. "When I have a day off," he says (and with Andre a free day is rare), "I go on the road. I may not run but walk for an hour at a time. That's all I need to get my wind back."

For relaxation Andre does enjoy one thing tremendously—going to the movies. But, of course, his choices are limited—for with his immense proportions there are places Andre simply cannot go, things he just cannot do.

The thing that Andre does do, *par excellence,* is wrestle. He is a master in that arena, a giant not only in size but also in skill. Once in the ring, he does only one thing, the thing he knows how to do best, the only thing he has ever done—win!

Spiros Arion

"Let me tell you one thing," he snarls. "The name of the game is money. And to make money you've gotta use bodies, you've gotta beat bodies. You've gotta be on top, and to do that you've gotta throw that rulebook away."

Surprising words from a professional athlete. But not so shocking when one realizes that the wrestler speaking is Spiros Arion.

The 268 pound Iron Greek has been at the top of the professional wrestling world for many years. In the beginning of his career he was respected as an incredibly talented

Spiros Arion (*Frank Amato*)

and knowledgeable scientific wrestler. He fought on tag teams with Bruno Sammartino and Chief Jay Strongbow. He and Sammartino were friends. When he appeared in the United States for the first time in 1973, he was instantly loved by all the fans. But then, in 1974, he went back to Greece for a short visit and returned to the United States a drastically changed man, a wrestler who had turned to the use of more questionable and aggressive tactics.

I remember seeing Arion wrestle many opponents in what I termed kicking matches. His technique was always the same. Once he gained the advantage over his opponent, he would beat upon him mercilessly, usually kicking him violently, far beyond the point necessary to win the match. Sometimes he would throw injured men off stretchers and kick them again.

Those black boots cut into abdomen after abdomen, with no degree of mercy. And always, egging him on outside the ring, was his manager, the man who made him "see the light"—the light of rulebreaking, that is—Fred Blassie.

"With the help of Fred Blassie, I'll get that World belt," he boasts. "All I need is myself and the brains behind me. That's Freddie Blassie."

Blassie, a onetime wrestler, is known for turning the heads of many scientific wrestlers to make them see the "advantages" in rulebending and sometimes brutal maneuvers.

But it is impossible to write about Spiros Arion without admitting that he is an enormously skillful wrestler. He has strength,

Opposite: Spiros Arion vs. Baron Mikel Scicluna (*Frank Amato*)

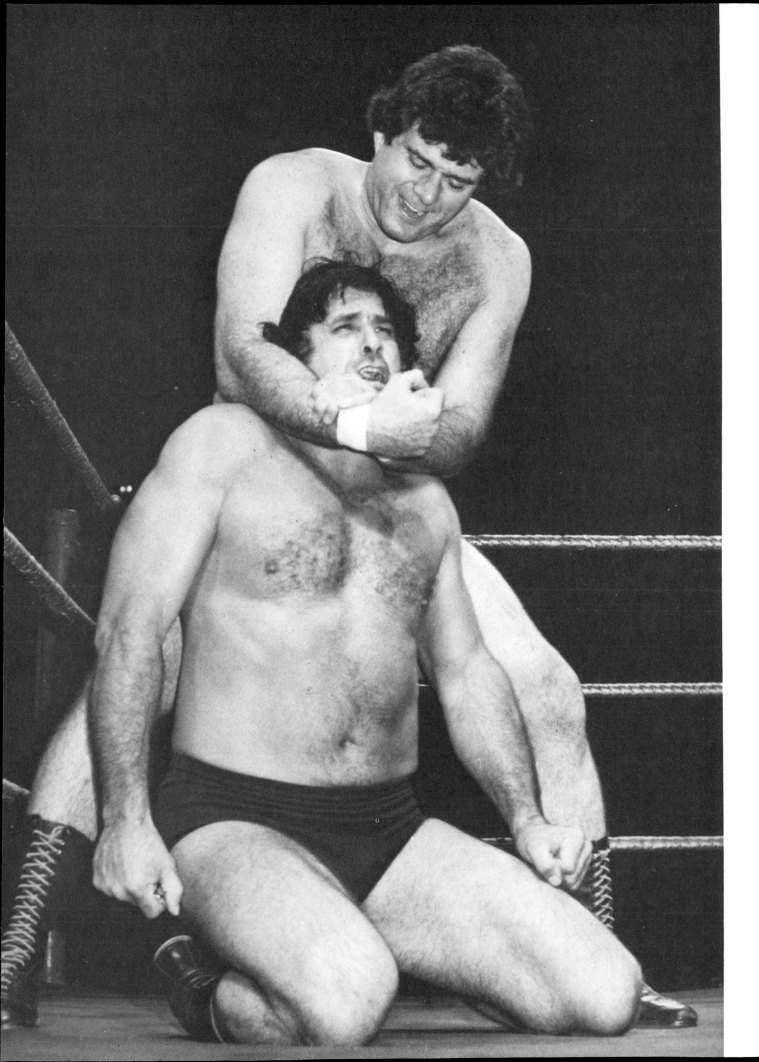

speed, and endurance. The talents are there even if the motives and methods are questionable.

"I don't care what people say about me," Arion says. "If they didn't like me, they wouldn't come. But they do come from coast to coast in America. I'm likeable, breaking rules or not breaking rules."

"Likeable" may not be the term that many would use, but Spiros is a popular wrestler. It is his skill and the excitement his power generates that make him a crowd favorite.

His haughty arrogance also goads fans on.

Because Spiros Arion is a trained athlete many thought, during his early years, that he could be an outstanding scientific champion. "I competed in the Olympic Games in Rome, 1960, as an amateur. I came in sixth. Then a year later I tried to become a professional wrestler, and I succeeded. I started in Paris." He goes on to advise young wrestlers to start with a solid amateur background. "To become a great professional you must first be a great amateur."

Spiros Arion vs. Dusty Rhodes (*Frank Amato*)

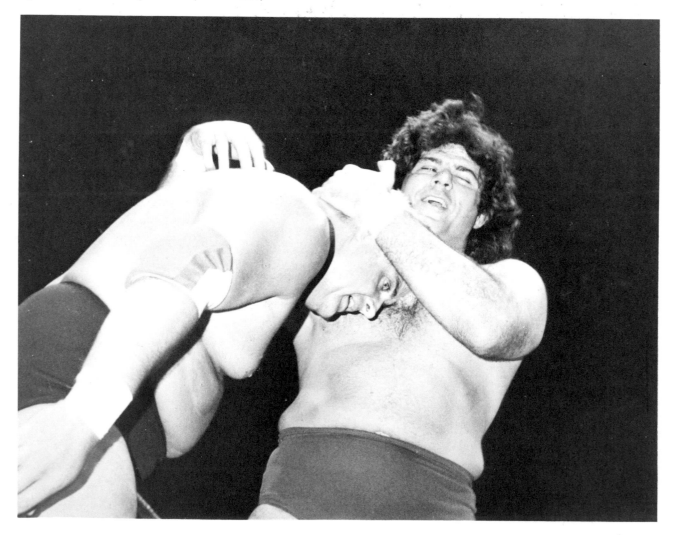

Arion has held many titles in the wrestling world, including the Austral-Asian Belt, the European Belt, and, in the early 1960s, the WWWF Tag Team Championship Belt. No one can question his ability or his athletic background.

"I love all kinds of sports. I run almost every day; 20 or 30 miles a week of running. I swim a lot, play racquetball, handball. . . ."

Arion is one of the few wrestlers who doesn't lift weights. "I'm always in good condition," he states firmly. "And I hate weights, because I believe that if you build big muscles you squash your brain."

The one thing Arion wants more than anything else is that championship belt, and he has fought for it many times. He claims that there is a "conspiracy" against his getting it but feels that in time he and Blassie will break through it. "I've been chasing that belt for the last 16 years. I'm gonna get it. I'm only 38. I'm still young. Jimmy Londos got it when he was 44. I'll get it way before that."

To say that Spiros Arion is a competitive wrestler would be a gross understatement. He considers everyone his enemy and respects no wrestlers other than himself. "I don't consider myself a great wrestler," he says with a mocking smile. "Know why? Because I'm the greatest."

I couldn't help smiling. He lurched forward, I jumped back. "Don't laugh," he stormed, waving his finger in my direction. "I am the greatest, and people know it. I've been chasing all professional wrestlers for 16 years. I'm not afraid, and I'll never be."

He softens when we talk about his family, his wife and three children, and when we talk about the sport in general, which he does love. He tells me how he's wrestled all over the world, in Europe, Asia, South Africa, Australia, and the Far East. "I never stop." He smiles proudly, folding his hands across his chest, a very self-satisfied man.

But Spiros Arion has one more point to make. "In wrestling," he starts, "nature has been very rude to me."

How so, Spiros? Because you haven't got that belt?

He shakes his head. "No. You know why I say this? Because she left me no room for improvement!"

I thought of the black boots of Spiros Arion connecting with their mark long after his opponents were down. No, the man does not know when to stop.

Bob Backlund

When you watch Bob Backlund in the ring, you know you are watching one of the most skillful and decent wrestlers around. The man from Princeton, Minnesota, has proven time and time again that he has the strength and stamina necessary to make a champion.

Bob Backlund won the World Wide Wrestling Federation Heavyweight Championship on February 20, 1978, in a controversial match with the man who held the belt at that time, Superstar Billy Graham. Many more experienced grapplers had tried to get the

Bob Backlund (*Frank Amato*)

belt away from Graham, but his brutal tactics and incredible strength always triumphed. So no one fully expected Backlund—one of the lightest (at 239 pounds) and youngest men in the sport—to do the job.

But along with stamina and strength Bob possesses amazing speed and agility. He has been wrestling since he was a boy, through high school and into college, and he represents the new breed of wrestlers, who are true athletes and thoroughly trained in the sport.

In the bout with Graham he matched him hold for hold, finally setting him up for what Bobby calls his atomic kneedrop, raising his opponent high in the air and dropping him onto his knee. Backlund fell over his man for the pin, and the count started. On the count of three Graham supposedly put his foot over the rope, but the referee did not see it. Backlund was declared the new champion, and Graham was livid, swearing that his belt had been stolen from him. (Despite the fact that Graham himself had won his own title controversially, when he pinned the Living Legend, Bruno Sammartino, using the bottom ropes for leverage and support out of range of the referee's vision.)

Tapes of the match were replayed, and Backlund, always a fair sportsman, agreed that a second match should take place. It did. In this match the fighting became more brutal, with Graham obviously out to give his young opponent a wrestling lesson. Backlund began to bleed quite a bit, and the referee stopped the match and awarded it to Graham. Of course, this did not mean that

Opposite: Bob Backlund vs. Superstar Billy Graham (*Frank Amato*)

Superstar could have his belt back, as that would have to have been done with a pin.

So the stage was set for one of the most exciting matches in wrestling history—the Steel-Cage Match between Bob Backlund and Superstar Billy Graham.

Graham was used to Steel-Cage Matches, in which both wrestlers are put into a 15-foot-high steel cage, with no time limit and no referee. The winner is the one who leaves the cage first. The danger of such a match lies in the fact that if the triumphant wrestler is vicious enough he may continue to beat his opponent mercilessly with no referee to stop him.

Backlund had never fought in this way before, and many doubted his ability to triumph over the experienced and ruthless Superstar. A record crowd of 26,000 came to view this bout at Madison Square Garden in New York.

After the tide had turned both ways several times during the match, Graham's leg became lodged in the steel, and Backlund left the cage, clearly winning in a little over 14 minutes of action and proving at last that he did deserve to wear that prestigious belt around his waist.

But Backlund still had a lot to prove to the crowds. He was a virtual newcomer in a sea of legends, having only made his first appearance in the Garden on September 26, 1977. People wondered if he was tough enough to meet the challenge of fighting each month to retain his belt. They knew that a whole lineup of the most brutal grapplers in the sport were out for his belt and for his blood, men with the experience he lacked. Was he really up to challenges like that?

Bob admits that before his bouts he was tense. "I'm always nervous before matches," he says. "I've never been in a match that I haven't worried about, no matter who it is. There's always somebody that could have that one chance of beating you. I've been nervous since I started wrestling at the age of 10, and every year I'd say, Maybe the next year it'll get better. But it didn't, it was getting worse and worse, and as the winnings keep getting more and more, the pressure gets more and more, and you get more nervous.

"I mean, there's a lot at stake, and anybody I wrestle shoots for me and for the title."

As for the criticisms hurled at him regarding his lack of experience, Bob has a logical answer: "They have to remember how old they were when they started wrestling. A lot of them were 20 years old. What I don't have in experience I try to gain in desire, because I've learned to be a winner and I hate to lose. That makes me drive myself just a little more."

Month after month, match after match, Backlund proved that even after only four years in professional wrestling he could beat the best. His finishing hold, the atomic kneedrop, soon became one of the most feared holds in the sport, and his knowledge of wrestling moves and maneuvers seemed unsurpassed. He trained fanatically for each match, watched films of each of his opponents in action, and knew how to counter any rotten trick they might have in store for him.

Interviewing Backlund is as enjoyable as watching his skill in the ring. He is a soft-spoken, polite young man, appreciative of his success and of his fans, humble but fearless, growing in confidence each day.

When asked about his chances of keeping the belt, he said, "I feel like I could beat just

Bob Backlund vs. Antonio Inoki (*Koichi*)

about anybody." He added, "I'll wrestle anybody, any place. . . . I love to wrestle, and I like the best competition there is."

And competition he gets. Besides appearing in packed Garden matches, he has met opponents all across the country and throughout the world. Men like Luke Graham, NWA champion Harley Race (in a match of the "belts" that ended in a draw), and even his old friend Chief Peter Maivia, who suddenly turned on Backlund in the middle of a match where they were tag team partners.

On the West Coast he has stunned fans with his skills, and he became a favorite in Japan when he wrestled the phenomenal Japanese champion, Antonio Inoki, to a one-hour draw, both wrestlers matching holds and excelling in their sport.

Of course, Bob owes a lot to his manager, Arnold Skaaland, the Golden Boy of Wrestling, who was responsible for helping and guiding another great, Bruno Sammartino. Skaaland advises Backlund on how to deal with each opponent, and the duo seems unbeatable.

As mentioned, Bob Backlund has been wrestling since he was a boy. In college he won All American honors four times, in addition to the prestigious National College Athletic Association (NCAA) title in 1971.

Backlund turned pro in 1974 and started wrestling in the AWA, where he was guided by such wrestling greats as Verne Gagne and Billy Robinson, among others. Soon after Bob went to Texas, he upset Terry Funk for the Western States Title. In Florida, his next stop, he teamed up with Steve Keirn, and together they won the Florida Tag Team Championship. When asked who he feels helped him the most in those early days, he says:

"When I started out, Danny Hodges helped me. He was a wrestler for about 15 years and a national champion. He turned me on to it considerably. The Funk brothers and Jack Brisco helped me a lot. Bruno Sammartino advised me somewhat. So there's been a lot of wrestlers out of college ranks that have helped me and pushed me along, and I guess I can say that they helped me considerably. But right now I can say that the fans have helped me most of all with their support.''

Many people comment on Backlund's incredible strength, which he tells me is primarily due to his mental attitude and wrestling skill. "There's knowing when to pick somebody up," he explains, "when it's easier to use his weight to his disadvantage and your advantage. Of course, there's a time when you have to be strong to pick someone up. But the kind of strength you need for wrestling isn't the kind of strength you need for weightlifting.''

He goes on to explain how technique is the whole key to winning matches, and he should know all about that. "Skill will outmatch strength. You can bring the strongest man in the world in the ring, and I could take him down with skill. You can't use your strength for a very long time because you're going to get tired. But if you use your skill and finesse you can keep on going.''

Bob's secret for success may lie in his dedication to training. He runs every day and goes to the gym at least four times a week to work with weight machines and practise holds and maneuvers. His discipline in this area is evident even when he is questioned about his leisure time activities.

"I have a good time when I'm training," he says. "I guess everybody else works on cars or watches TV, but my hobby is training, working out. It relaxes me as much as anything.''

Bob's other outside activities include playing tennis, racquetball, and volleyball, shooting pool, bowling, and listening to music (especially country and Western music). He also tries to spend as much time as he can with his wife and young daughter. He enjoys the outdoors. "I'm not a hunter or a fisherman," he says. "I'd rather go out and look at nature than go out and kill.''

Though Bobby prides himself on wrestling clean, on being a scientific grappler, his opponents normally do not. And injuries are a problem. "Back injuries have been the worst," Backlund admits. "They don't recover as fast as some of the other injuries. Just about everybody in professional wrestling has some kind of bad back.''

But no injury seems to stop the young champion, and one of the most exciting things about his matches is watching the extraordinary beatings and punishment he can take and still retain his strength, coming back to overcome his surprised opponent and make that pin.

"I like to go in there and think that I could wrestle and wrestle clean, but I know my opponents pretty well by the time I go into the ring. I watch their performance style. I know what they're going to try to do to me. I guess I kind of expect it." Bob enjoys wrestling clean grapplers like Jack Brisco, but he knows that with most of his opponents "people are just after whatever the object may be, a title or money, I guess," and he is the target.

Bobby has a true sportsman's attitude when it comes to his opponents. I asked him to name some of the greatest wrestlers around. "Well, I respect them all," he said sincerely. "I don't like some of the things they do, but I respect them. I respect Tony Garea, Larry Zbyszko, Dusty Rhodes. I also respect Superstar Billy Graham, Ivan Koloff, and Spiros Arion. Of those last few names, I don't like the way they wrestle, but I still respect their abilities."

Bob Backlund's life has changed a lot since winning the WWWF championship, as it was bound to do. He gets tougher and rougher opponents now, and spends a great deal of time traveling, in the United States and throughout the world. Another thing that's changed his life, he says, is "interest in me in the street, the publicity. My family has changed," he adds. "My income has gone up considerably since I won the title. I guess that in itself changes your whole lifestyle."

In his position he sometimes finds it hard "to trust anybody." But his fans are certainly behind him; he can be sure of that. For when Bob first arrived in the WWWF areas, he couldn't get any matches. Managers were keeping their grapplers from meeting this new superstar. He credits his fans with breaking the boycott. "The fans wrote in a lot of letters, and they really helped me get into this area, they helped me to get the matches I needed."

For one of the newest men in professional wrestling, Bob Backlund, the All-American, has certainly charged right to the top, proving his determination beyond a doubt. He probably summed it up best, explaining how he charges around the ring like a flash, slips and spins out of painful holds, and fights against great odds until no opponent can safely feel he can be kept down, by stating simply, confidently, "I like to win."

Bob Backlund vs. Ivan Koloff (*Frank Amato*)

Nick Bockwinkle

If you ran a contest to select the most popular, congenial, and fair athlete in professional wrestling Nick Bockwinkle certainly wouldn't win it. However, if the contest was for an impressive number of victories or for learning and erudition he might pull it off.

On November 8, 1975, Nick Bockwinkle won the AWA Heavyweight Championship in a very controversial match against the great Minnesota mat king, Verne Gagne. Since that time many people have said that Nick's inhumanity has brought disgrace to the belt he wears.

He is 250 pounds of mean machine, and there is no trick in the book that is too vicious for him to use. Although he is considered a master of the subtle rulebreaking moves, Bockwinkle is no improviser in the ring. He is guided in all his endeavors by his superambitious manager, Bobby "the Brain" Heenan, and carefully maps out all his strategies with Heenan before each match. In fact, some feel that Bockwinkle would be nothing without Heenan.

Bockwinkle was formerly the AWA Tag Team Champion with his ex-friend, Ray Stevens, who is now a hated rival. Nick's father, Warren, was also a wrestler, and many years ago they wrestled together in tag team bouts. His dad has since retired.

Although Bockwinkle is a man with few friends and scores of fans who taunt him every time he steps into the ring, it doesn't seem to bother him. He is only impressed with his victories and his paycheck. "Actually, I prefer nobody," he says flat out. "I would just like to collect my money and be left alone."

The first thing that strikes you about Nick Bockwinkle is the way he expresses himself, which sometimes borders on brilliance. He is a learned, complex man who enjoys speaking at colleges and being taunted in verbal bouts he claims he always wins. Even when the subject of rulebreaking comes up, he has a logical way of excusing it.

"We're going to have to more delicately define the term 'rulebreakers,' " he begins. "Like pulling hair, pulling trunks, well in some states you have three or four seconds to stop that pulling or using the butt of the hand instead of the forearm. Now if I do anything like that in less than three or four seconds, I'm within the rules. If you really made the rules so incredibly stringent it would be a matter of blowing the whistle all the time."

Flagrant rulebreaking, however, such as using foreign objects, even Nick does not support. "When you're really flagrant, you're not wrestling. These people are doing what they're doing because they don't have the ability. They're admitting they're short on talent."

Bockwinkle would never admit that himself. Modesty is not one of his virtues. He does admit, however, that he isn't perfect, even after 15 years in professional wrestling. "I'm one of the best," he says, "and I'm still learning."

Nick was helped into the pro ring by his father. "It was something that happened after getting busted up playing college football, and he said to me, 'Well, you didn't produce too well these first couple of years. . . .' I had a sharp father, and I anticipated it. So he started training me, and I wrestled through my last couple of years in college."

Though Nick sometimes claims he should

Nick Bockwinkle

be given all three belts, he does have praise for other wrestlers. Asked who he thinks are the best, he begins with his old rival. "Verne Gagne. He's always been a scrambler and will be till the day he dies. Terry Funk, the former NWA champion. Goodness, this fellow the Crusher, from Milwaukee. And there's Andre the Giant, who pushes you right to the limit."

He goes on to praise the skills of Dick the Bruiser and Billy Robinson while telling me that he considers Mad Dog Vachon the most vicious man in the ring. "Mad Dog is every bit as flagrant and outlandish in real life as he is in the ring. His name is apropos. He really is a disparate individual of extremes, an unbelievable and off-the-wall personality."

Bockwinkle assures me that he welcomes good competition as much as he likes winning. "Give me the greatest challengers ever," he states. "That way, I am able to produce my very best, and that makes the brightest shining moment in one's career important, so that if someone is very good and can take you almost to the very edge of the cliff, without getting you pushed over, he's made you perform your best."

Nick wrestles mainly on the West Coast but certainly has a reputation throughout the United States. He tells me that he is a "pretty positive-thinking individual" who is still "thrilled" when he wins matches. He speaks of his hobbies—photography and making furniture—and the other sports he enjoys—fishing, tennis, paddleball, hiking, surfing, and skiing. It's obvious that Bockwinkle is a man of boundless energy both in and outside of the ring.

He is also a philosopher. Nick Bockwinkle on professional wrestling is a fascinating course of study. He tells me first that he loves the fans and wishes "there were ten million more," then goes on to analyze what makes a wrestling enthusiast and why he thinks the sport is so popular.

"Wrestling is an enigmatic thing," he says thoughtfully. "People can be linked to it. There is a Latin expression, *flagrante delicto*—in the heat of passion. The passion of a wrestling match can mean love. The basic down-to-earth, sensual humanness about the body. It can be flying around, crashing into each other. I think that's a lot of what the appeal is. It can be tied down to a certain degree of our animal instincts."

He goes on to comment on the need for civilized savagery, for violence of this athletic nature. "There is something about violence. Maybe you got knocked out sometime in your life. Regardless of the circumstance there is that deep feeling. There is that physical, mental, spiritual awareness of life. It happens enough in sports. You realize how alive you are at that moment."

I pulled him back to wrestling itself, though I hated to. For whatever Nick is called in the ring, he is obviously respected for his mind by many people outside of it. I asked him what his favorite holds were, and he became his old self. "Anything that will bring victory!"

Bockwinkle has dished out injuries by his tactics, but he has received many as well. "How long is the tape?" he jokingly asked, wondering if we would run out of time if he listed them all. "I've had a broken leg, several knee operations, a dislocated shoulder, elbows, broken ribs, a bad back, ten thousand sore muscles, broken joints. . . ."

Nick Bockwinkle is certainly a veteran of the ring. His dreaded piledriver has finished off many an opponent when his other tactics haven't done the job already. And he is proud of his abilities and does believe that he gets good competition. He attributes all his victories to his outlook on life.

THE STARS

''Mechanically speaking, on any given day, myself, Robinson, Gagne, Sammartino, Funk, to name a few, we're all pretty much on a par. With myself, I try to realize that, forget about the mechanical aspect of the thing, realize that the secret's in the whole mental aspect of it.''

Nick Bockwinkle certainly has a handle on both the mental and mechanical aspects of wrestling. Though many people hate the idea, it doesn't look as though Bockwinkle could ever be anywhere but at the top, no matter how he does it.

Dino Bravo

Another member of the new breed of college-trained wrestlers is the very talented Dino Bravo. His scientific perfection and high sense of fair play have made him one of the most popular athletes in the World Wide Wrestling Federation and in all the other areas around the United States and Canada.

A native of Montreal, Canada, Dino weighs 248 pounds and is in superb physical condition at all times. "I like to have a lot of speed

Dino Bravo (*Frank Amato*)

and surprise my opponent by using a lot of powerful stuff," he says. "I like to keep my strength way up, and then I feel I'm stronger than I ever was before."

No one can deny Dino Bravo's strength and speed. In addition to being a superstar in wrestling, he once chalked up 69 consecutive victories, all in under 15 minutes.

Dino began his wrestling career in 1974 in Canada, where he fought for three years. He then moved on to Los Angeles, where he immediately captured the Americas tag team title with Victor Rivera and successfully defended it for quite some time. After that he won the International Wrestling Association (IWA) tag team title with another friend from Montreal, Gino Brito, and at the same time was awarded the title Rookie of the Year.

Bravo moved to the Mid-Atlantic area, where he consistently defeated all major opponents. Here he also captured a tag team title with Mr. Wrestling while forming an intense rivalry with the vicious Ric Flair, whom he finds it difficult to talk about even today.

Bravo was by now recognized as a major new force in professional wrestling. After finally dropping the title with Mr. Wrestling, he went to Georgia, where he also met with instant success. All these victories convinced him to try his skill in the WWWF.

Almost six weeks to the day after Dino Bravo entered the World Wide Wrestling Federation he teamed up with a good friend and fine wrestler, Domenic DeNucci, and these two powerhouses captured the WWWF Tag Team Championship.

Dino was somewhat frustrated by his constant placement in tag teams, knowing by

Opposite: Dino Bravo vs. Luke Graham (*Frank Amato*)

now that he could fare well in individual competition. So that the tragedy which finally struck Bravo and DeNucci, when the ruthless Lumberjacks took their title from them on June 26, 1978, with many illegal maneuvers, turned out to be something of a blessing in disguise for young Dino Bravo.

Now he was on his own. Could he do as well as his wrestling history seemed to indicate he would? Without a doubt! The technically exact and powerful style of Dino Bravo again literally swept his opponents off their feet.

Defeating men like Stan Stasiak, Butcher Vachon, and Luke Graham, all in under 15 minutes, was no small task, but Dino handled it with ease. His flying dropkick was considered throughout the wrestling world to be as devastating to feel as it was exciting to watch. And one of his finishing moves, the airplane spin, in which he lifts his opponent up on his back and spins him rapidly around, left many a more experienced competitor dazed and defeated.

Along with Bravo's wrestling excellence goes a driving ambition, and he is determined to win a world championship belt—or retire. "I set myself a goal, and if I don't accomplish it in the next few years, well, then I'm just going to quit. I'm not going to take a back seat in anything I do."

Dino Bravo is an all-around athlete. "I was involved in track and field throughout high school and college, and I really enjoyed running and sprinting and the high jump . . . and the pole vault. I think you've got to be in top physical shape to compete in any kind of track and field event. That really helped me through my wrestling, because I was always in good shape. I really had to push myself, keep my weight down, work on my speed and reflex rate."

A dedicated trainer who works out in the gym all week, he started wrestling when he was nine years old.

"I never thought I'd become a professional, but my cousin, Louis Cerdan, was a professional wrestler and really pushed me into it. He asked me to try it, and I did, and I did well on my first match. I loved every minute of it."

Bravo has no fear when it comes to taking on rough opponents and rulebreakers. He says, "I'm really looking for tough competition." A man like Dino, with his loyalty and fine sense of sportsmanship, often finds himself in the ring with a rulebreaker. But Dino believes that even these overly aggressive grapplers have their place in wrestling: "It gets people angry when they see a guy break the rules, but that, I think, is a really important part of wrestling. I mean, it may sound funny to say it, but if not for the rulebreakers, maybe there would be less people in the arenas."

Actually that is a very brave attitude, for although Dino is lightning quick and seldom gives his opponent the chance to get an advantage, he has been hurt. "I tore a tendon in my right shoulder," he remembers. "It was the most painful of injuries you can get. It's worse than a fracture and it takes forever to heal . . . but I woke up one day, and God bless me, the pain was gone, and I went back to the gym." But it took over a year and a half for that injury to heal completely!

Dino's favorite wrestler is unquestionably Bruno Sammartino, with whom he would even fight on a tag team, though he now avoids tag team competition.

Bravo admits to being nervous before matches. "I think that makes me a little better, because I go in there and I'm really cautious. Before I compete, I'm a nervous wreck."

But the grappler has his way of relaxing.

Dino Bravo vs. Superstar Billy Graham (*Frank Amato*)

"My favorite hobby, and it might sound funny, is horse racing. I love harness racing, and that's one kind of competition too. I love to see horses run. Every time I get a day off, I go to the closest track."

Anyone who has seen Dino at work, with his flying head scissors, takedowns, dropkicks, suplexes, or airplane spins, knows the man has nothing to fear. "I feel sometimes, when I feel good, that I could tear a guy's head off his shoulders if I can really get up there," he says, referring to those incredible dropkicks.

So the rulebreakers do have a lot to fear from the likes of Dino Bravo. He wants people like Superstar Billy Graham, Ivan Koloff, Ernie Ladd, and other awesome competitors to know he is ready for them all. "I wish I could talk in public here so they could hear it now. I'd like to wrestle them anywhere, any time, any place. Whenever they want to choose it, I'll be there to do it."

Dino Bravo is not only a new wrestling superstar, he is also one of the fans' favorites. And the feeling is mutual: "A lot of times I win matches because of the fans, because they kind of push you so much. And when you know they're behind you that much, you just make it a must to win matches.

"The fans have been great to me over the seven years I've been wrestling, and they're the reason I'm still a wrestler, because it's just great to go out there and feel the people are with you. It's like a home team in football. They always play better in front of their fans. It causes you to put in an extra effort, and it makes you . . . the winner."

Wrestling fans all over the country agree with Dino Bravo. He is a winner.

Jack Brisco

Former NWA champion Jack Brisco is included in almost every list of the very top men in the professional wrestling world. He also ranks high on the list of the fairest grapplers, the most decent sportsmen in the ring—men with skill and strength who do not normally need to resort to rulebreaking to win their matches.

Brisco is a true professional who conducts himself with dignity in every situation.

Jack Brisco (*Frank Amato*)

He possesses incredible concentration and precision when facing opponents and a steely strength that often intimidates them. His figure-four leglock has devastated many a man, as has his amazing agility, which gives rise to a wide variety of skillful speed maneuvers.

Jack Brisco is always in excellent physical condition, which accounts for his stamina in the ring. He is still going strong long after his opponent has reached the point of near-surrender.

The 232-pound grappler from Blackwell, Oklahoma, has been wrestling for 13 years. "I wrestled in high school," he tells me. "Then I won a scholarship to wrestle at Oklahoma State University. After that I decided to become a professional, when I came out of college. Leo McGurk, a promoter in Oklahoma, helped me turn pro and gave me a contract."

Since that time Jack has met scores of rough opponents, among them Harley Race, Bobby Duncum, and Blackjack Lanza. Brisco won his NWA heavyweight title from Harley Race in July 1973 in Texas. He later lost it on December 10, 1975, to Terry Funk. He makes it plain that he would like that title back, and many people feel he could easily have it.

Jack does a lot of wrestling in tag team competition with his brother Jerry, and together they have won such titles as the Florida Tag Team Championship. They are close, both as brothers and as wrestlers, and their styles admirably complement each other.

Jack Brisco says that Eddie Graham is the man who helped him most in professional wrestling. "After I turned pro," he says, "he was more or less my coach. I became successful under his guidance." Brisco says that because he is much smaller than many other grapplers he relies on quickness. "I don't do any weightlifting," he explains. "I do a lot of swimming, long-distance running, and stretching exercises."

Jack is definitely a scientific wrestler and doesn't care for rulebreaking. "They need to tighten up the rules in this sport," he comments, and most would agree with him.

His favorite opponent, or rather the man he most enjoys wrestling as a creditable challenge to his skills, is Terry Funk's brother, Dory Funk, Jr., whom he considers a fine and capable contender.

Jack, who has always been popular with his fans, tells me how much he appreciates their support. He also speaks of the "self-satisfaction" he gets out of competing on the mat. "I'm a little bit excited, nervous, before a match. But if I win I always feel good."

When Jack Brisco wins, everyone in the arena also feels good. His performance in the ring is always a first-rate lesson in how to be a skillful and decent wrestler, and he is also a man who brings honor and credit to his sport wherever he goes.

Jack Brisco vs. Terry Funk (*Frank Amato*)

Verne Gagne

In 1958 Edouard Carpentier, the Flying Frenchman, was defeated in a match against Verne Gagne. Gagne, now a champion in a group which had splintered away from the National Wrestling Alliance, finally decided to settle the question of who was the world's champion by issuing a challenge

Verne Gagne (*Frank Amato*)

to the then-formal NWA champ, Pat O'Connor. O'Connor did not respond. So on August 16, 1960, Verne Gagne was declared the American Wrestling Association (AWA) Champion.

Today, after an incredible 30-year career on the mat, Verne Gagne is dedicated to helping future champions get their start and to furthering the sport he has devoted so much of his life to. And he is still in the ring, as skillful and full of stamina as ever.

Gagne is recognized by many as the expert on the intricacies of scientific wrestling. He is a tireless trainer who keeps in supreme condition at all times. Young men like Rick Steamboat and Bob Backlund praise him for all the help he has given young grapplers on their way up in the sport, and his own son, Greg, is recognized as an excellent athlete and a top contender for the AWA championship belt.

"I'm a basic wrestler," Verne tells me. "I enjoy the sport, and I have been doing it for many years. It'll be 30 years on May 10 of 1979, and I was wrestling in amateur competition for 7 years. I still enjoy it. I've seen all aspects, basically, of wrestling, both on professional and amateur levels. I think my technique now is as good as it's ever been."

No doubt about it. Verne Gagne is still a master of the mat and wouldn't mind winning back the AWA title he last lost to Nick Bockwinkle on November 8, 1975. Many feel he could do it.

Verne Gagne is from Minneapolis, Minnesota, and weighs 230 pounds. He tells me how he first got into professional wrestling. "I wrestled in high school, and I was the champion here in Minnesota. Then I went to the University of Minnesota, and I played football and wrestled there. . . . I was National Collegiate Champion and National AAU Champion. I was also on the Olympic Team.

"I don't think any one person helps you get to the top. There was a series of events. When you're in amateur wrestling, it's your coach that helps you the most. And professionally . . . I had fellows like some of the pros I worked out with before I became a professional . . . that helped a great deal. Joe Peszedaki was one of them. I started my professional career here in Minneapolis under the guidance of a fellow by the name of Tony Stecker, and Wally Karbo."

He tells me how he got his first real break around 1951, when he appeared out of Chicago on the old Dumont TV network. "I got on the rest of the network, which at that time covered three quarters of America. I did really well there. And financially I guess I was able to realize some of my dreams—so it all worked out really well."

Since Verne Gagne knows so much about the sport and has seen it change over the years, I asked his opinion on how it could be improved. "There's a lot of ways to improve it," he suggests. "And that's in America. Number one . . . tighten up on the rules and have a uniform set of rules so everybody basically knows what breaking the rules of wrestling is. And then, the wrestlers themselves. By training. Some people just train tremendously, like Bob Backlund. A lot of the young people are really hard trainers. When I first came into wrestling, I don't think people trained that much. But then still . . . you'll see the fat guy who can't really produce in the ring, and he doesn't train."

He believes, however, that wrestling is getting "bigger and better than ever." Many people feel that Verne Gagne is one of the people responsible for that. "We're getting better athletes," he comments. "You see more action because they move quicker. The future looks bright for professional wrestling. And I think by the continuous support of the fans wrestling grows. In some places in the United States it's just booming."

It's easy to see what a large part the sport plays in Verne Gagne's life—in the ring as well as outside it. He is still adept at the many holds and maneuvers he has developed over the years—probably none of them so devastating as his famous sleeper hold, which sends his opponent off for a nap. "I dropkick, as well," he says. "But the sleeper and the dropkicks are more flashy holds." He adds that basic wrestling knowledge has always been the thing he relies on.

"When you come out tired after a good wrestling match, against a good opponent, I mean a man who strictly wrestles, and not the rough stuff but the clean wrestling . . . well, it's great, you know you've been against a great opponent and you've had a good match."

Verne has met some rough opponents over the years. Aggressiveness is not a trait he is known for; he always tries to keep his temper and his dignity in the ring. But he has been injured by more vicious opponents. He recalls an incident that was particularly serious. "Last year I had a man kneedrop me on my ear. They closed the canal off—cauliflowered, you know what that is. I had to have surgery and was out for three months." He finds it a relief after a match when he doesn't "come out beaten up or hurt. You know, if you're not injured you feel terrific."

He adds, "You come out of every match a different way."

He still admits to being nervous before a

Following two pages: Verne Gagne vs. Nikolai Volkoff (*George Napolitano*)

match, and that is probably because he takes his sport seriously. He only wrestles in main events and tells me that he gets the best of opponents. He feels that one of the greatest men he's ever wrestled against is Billy Robinson and that his most vicious opponents have been Hans Schmidt and Mad Dog Vachon.

Verne Gagne has many outside interests. "I do a lot of bird hunting, water skiing, and snow skiing. We go to Aspen and places like that . . . do a lot of hunting in South Dakota, Canada, and Nebraska. And I fly an airplane." He also raises quarter horses which his daughter, Donna, shows. They have taken prizes at the New York State Fair, the Indiana Fair, and the Minnesota State Fair.

To train, Verne Gagne lifts weights, plays tennis, and runs. And of course he wrestles. He is called by many the Dean of Scientific Wrestling.

When asked about who he would select as a tag team partner, he again cites Billy Robinson and an obvious choice, his son Greg, who is rising fast in the wrestling world.

But in a way Greg is not the only son Verne Gagne has in professional wrestling, although he is the only one related by blood. The others are the scores of young men Verne has inspired or helped to reach the top ranks of the sport, a sport he has aided in every way he could.

He speaks about the kind of excitement he feels after having a good match. "You know you've not only enjoyed it, but the public has enjoyed it. The people who are there that watch it on television or at the arenas. That's a great satisfaction."

Verne Gagne has been giving that kind of satisfaction to people and they have been supporting him in kind ever since the famous day when the first AWA belt was placed around his waist.

Verne Gagne vs. Nikolai Volkoff (*George Napolitano*)

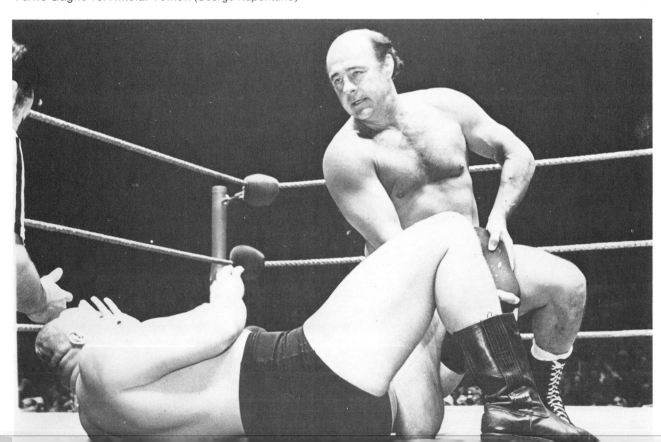

THE STARS

A Brief History of Verne Gagne, AWA Title Holder

DATE	WINNER	OPPONENT DEFEATED	LOCATION
Aug. 1958	VERNE GAGNE	Edouard Carpentier	Omaha
Nov. 1958	WILBUR SNYDER	Verne Gagne	Omaha
Feb. 26, 1960	VERNE GAGNE	Doctor X (Bill Miller)	Omaha

In the match with Gagne, Doctor X was not unmasked and the title did not change hands.
On Aug. 16, 1960, the Minneapolis program announced Verne Gagne as AWA champion.

Aug. 20, 1960	VERNE GAGNE	Doctor X (Bill Miller)	Omaha

The Aug. 20th bout was a Death Match. Doctor X was unmasked, but the title did not change hands.

Aug. 8, 1961	VERNE GAGNE	Gene Kiniski	Minneapolis
Sep. 16, 1961	VERNE GAGNE	Don Leo Jonathan	Omaha
Jan. 9, 1962	MISTER M (BILL MILLER)	Verne Gagne	Minneapolis
Jul. 21, 1962	FRITZ VON ERICH	Verne Gagne	Omaha
Aug. 21, 1962	VERNE GAGNE	Mister M (Bill Miller)	Minneapolis
Aug. 25, 1962	VERNE GAGNE	Fritz Von Erich	Omaha
Feb. 15, 1963	CRUSHER LISOWSKI	Verne Gagne	Omaha
Jul. 9, 1963	CRUSHER LISOWSKI	Verne Gagne	Minneapolis
Jul. 20, 1963	VERNE GAGNE	Crusher Lisowski	Minneapolis
Jul. 27, 1963	FRITZ VON ERICH	Verne Gagne	Omaha
Aug. 8, 1963	VERNE GAGNE	Fritz Von Erich	Amarillo
Sep. 7, 1963	VERNE GAGNE	Fritz Von Erich	Omaha
Nov. 28, 1963	CRUSHER LISOWSKI	Verne Gagne	St. Paul
Dec. 14, 1963	VERNE GAGNE	Crusher Lisowski	Minneapolis
May 2, 1964	MAD DOG VACHON	Verne Gagne	Omaha
May 16, 1964	VERNE GAGNE	Mad Dog Vachon	Omaha
Oct. 20, 1964	MAD DOG VACHON	Verne Gagne	Minneapolis
Feb. 26, 1967	VERNE GAGNE	Mad Dog Vachon	St. Paul
Aug. 17, 1968	DOCTOR X (DICK BEYERS)	Verne Gagne	Bloomington
Aug. 31, 1968	VERNE GAGNE	Doctor X (Dick Beyers)	Minneapolis
Nov. 8, 1975	NICK BOCKWINKLE	Verne Gagne	St. Paul

Tony Garea

Tony Garea, the talented and skillful grappler from Auckland, New Zealand, embodies a code of decency in the ring. At 240 pounds, 6 feet 1 inch, he is a powerhouse of knowledge and a favorite of the fans. Especially the women fans, who find him very attractive.

The Garea charm is never absent except in the ring, where it is replaced with determined ability. Almost from the start Tony has been at the top of the mat world, holding various tag team championships and coming close on many occasions to winning the world championship belt.

Tony Garea (*Frank Amato*)

Tony Garea started wrestling in 1971. "Originally, back home, I played rugby," he explains. "I played rugby all my life. I started when I was 5 years old. When I was 18, I moved up to the senior competition, and I was one of the first players to combine weightlifting, or weight-training, with rugby.

"A promoter from New Zealand heard about me, and he asked me if I'd like to train to wrestle professionally. I had done a little amateur wrestling with my cousin, who was the heavyweight champion of Auckland for a long time, so I knew a bit about it anyway."

The first place Tony wrestled in the United States was Tampa, Florida, in March 1972. The late Bobby Shane was his first opponent, and though Tony was beaten, he learned a lot from that bout about pro wrestling. Back home, he was used to more science and less fast, sometimes violent action. But he learned quickly and soon began to triumph over opponents like Dick Murdoch and Paul Jones.

Speaking now about rulebreakers, Tony is philosophical. "That's their style of wrestling," he says, shaking his head slightly, "and I think in professional wrestling you have an opportunity. It's one of the few sports where you can release the true 'you.' I think those guys who break the rules, well, if they could break the rules all their life and get away with it, they would. But they *can* do it in the ring to a certain degree." He adds, "Let them break a few rules . . . and I'll start breaking some myself."

Tony has been known on several occasions to lose his temper with violent rulebreakers. He is Irish on his mother's side,

Opposite: Tony Garea vs. Victor Rivera (*Frank Amato*)

Tony Garea vs. Gashouse Gilbert (*Frank Amato*)

and his temper is most effective when it explodes. I remember him chasing George Steele down the aisle of Madison Square Garden with the implement he had just wrenched from the Animal's hand.

When questioned about vicious wrestlers, Tony also remembers Steele. "George Steele comes to mind right away, because he's laid a chair across my arm when I was on the floor. He's laid a table across the back of my head. Anything that's around, he'll pick up and use."

Garea's record in the wrestling world shows he is one of the top men in the ring. In addition to holding the New Zealand Junior Heavyweight Championship Belt and the South Pacific Junior Heavyweight Championship, Tony won the WWWF Tag Team Championship, first in August 1973 with partner Haystacks Calhoun, then in December 1973 with Dean Ho, and again in December 1978 with Larry Zbyszko. He has shown his skills and stamina time and time again against all the top opponents. His battles with Superstar Billy Graham when Graham was champion are memorable.

I asked him who he thought the best wrestlers around were. "One man that helped me a lot and whom I've admired is Jack Brisco," he says, "and I watched Jack and Dory Funk, Jr., in some great matches in Florida. I was in California and in the WWWF with Pedro Morales, who's a great wrestler. And Bruno, of course, is one of the all time greats."

Tony intends to train for a little while before shooting again for the heavyweight championship belt. He had several injuries when he was fighting in Australia and New Zealand and wants to feel in top shape first. He reminds me that a champion must always be in excellent form, as he has to defend his title maybe twice a week on the average, 12 months a year.

Tony Garea's wrestling knowledge is extensive. He uses a wide variety of maneuvers and holds in the ring and is always sure of his abilities. "I like to use armlocks, top wristlocks, hammerlocks, front facelocks . . . but my finishing hold, when I can use it, is the abdominal stretch. The thing I like about the abdominal stretch is that as long as you've got it applied properly, you can lose your balance and go down and you still have it on. There's really no way you can lose if you've applied it right."

Tony Garea is very popular with the crowds, and he appreciates their support. But he feels the need to tell them not to touch or disturb wrestlers when they're leaving the ring. He explains that some grapplers have super-quick reflexes, and if they are smacked from behind they may instinctively turn around and defend themselves.

He also explains that wrestlers are afraid of overzealous fans who have grudges against certain grapplers. "One wrestler was split, in Boston, with a knife, from the knee to the hip," he says softly.

Garea, who has nothing of this sort to fear from the fans, is really saying this out of consideration for his fellow athletes—further evidence of what a decent and loyal sportsman he really is.

Superstar Billy Graham

What can you say about a man who's perfect? Or at least who *believes* he is. Well, one thing you can't say about this man is that he's modest.

The famous Graham family of wrestlers produced a whole breed of winners in the 1950s and '60s. Dr. Jerry and Eddie Graham held many belts, and when Eddie left the team in 1963, he was replaced by his brother Luke, also a fearless and skillful grappler. But in 1969 Dr. Jerry Graham showed up at a match with another member of the family at his side. This time it was his youngest brother, the one they called Superstar Billy Graham.

Superstar Billy Graham (*George Napolitano*)

Billy lived up to his name. In Baltimore, Maryland, on April 30, 1977, he did something many wrestlers had tried and failed to do. He defeated Bruno Sammartino and became the World Wide Wrestling Federation Heavyweight Champion.

While champion he defended the belt constantly, sometimes up to six times a week. He triumphed over men like Tony Garea, Chief Jay Strongbow, Bobo Brazil, Ivan Putski, and Gorilla Monsoon. With his combination of phenomenal strength and ruthless tactics, he looked unbeatable. Billy was never a modest man, and wearing the belt fueled his ego even more. "I am the greatest. The man with the power," he said. "I showed them all that my knowledge and ability was too great for them."

The match with Sammartino for the belt was a controversial one. Billy supposedly used the ropes for leverage in pinning his man, but the referee did not spot it. He met Sammartino on several other occasions, and the great Bruno tried to even the score and regain his belt, but Superstar always kept it out of his grasp.

People started to feel that the Superstar could not be beaten. But as fate would have it, on February 20, 1978, his belt was taken from him in another controversial match with scientific wrestler Bob Backlund. Backlund won the pin when Graham's leg was supposedly over the rope on the count of three. At Billy's insistence they fought two times after that to clear up the confusion. In the end Backlund won again, in a Steel-Cage Match, and kept his belt.

Graham maintains to this day that Back-

Opposite: Superstar Billy Graham vs. Bob Backlund (*George Napolitano*)

lund cheated and stole the belt from him. He vows revenge. "I'm determined to get back my belt and get that skinny punk's hide," he says, narrowing his eyes in a determined glare.

I asked Billy how coming from a family of great wrestlers had affected him. "Well, it really doesn't matter," he said, "because I outshine all of them so much. My brothers are great in their own right, but they can't compare to me."

He claims that no one helped him succeed in professional wrestling. "Nobody helped me to the top. I helped myself."

Billy Graham is famous for his strength and fanatic dedication to training, which he does "seven days a week." His 23-inch arms and 56-inch chest are a tremendous source of pride to him. In fact, one of his first titles was Mr. Teenage America, which he won on Muscle Beach in California. He is a dedicated bodybuilder, who says, "This beautiful body is my temple." Weightlifting is, of course, his other favorite sport.

Billy Graham comes from Paradise Valley, Arizona, where he lives today. His home is decorated in Indian style, and he loves Western art. "I go to museums a lot, as I appreciate art very much."

Many people disagree about the state of Billy's "art" in the ring. Although he is a rulebender, he has managed to stay very popular with the fans, probably because of his skill, strength, and colorful personality. He describes his style of grappling as "an exciting style, not a boring style, one that works. My style puts me on top, as a star. It's a style that fans love to see. The fans don't come to see amateur collegiate wrestling— they come to see different styles and techniques. They're entertained by this, and I'm a master of it."

One is impressed by Billy's confidence, fearlessness, and strong sense of identity. "You have to accomplish something for yourself. Nobody else can do it for you." On this score I can agree with him.

He loves wrestling because it is a confident man's sport. "The financial situation is very good for top wrestlers in the world. It's a very entertaining and independent sport. You're an individual, you're not on a team. Whatever you accomplish you do it on your own."

"I'm an individual," he adds. That's obvious by now.

Billy Graham says that there's "only a handful of wrestlers today of my caliber." He feels that Sammartino is tougher competition than Bob Backlund and that his toughest opponents have been Andre the Giant, Sammartino, and the American Dream, Dusty Rhodes.

Rhodes is the man he most enjoys wrestling, and the two have been feuding for quite a long time. In a recent Texas Bull-Rope Match Graham lost to Rhodes, but not before both wrestlers had become tired and bloody. Billy can hold his own against most any opponent.

Given a choice, Billy said, he would pick Andre the Giant as a tag team partner. That puzzled me, because Billy and Andre are not the best of friends. But Billy likes to win. To win, you would choose Andre.

"Wouldn't you?" he asks. At 91 pounds, I can't see myself having to make the decision. But I must agree with him. It is a good choice.

He still itches to get into the ring with Sammartino. "We're both powerful men," he explains. "It's just a magnetism between us both, so that is the perfect match, the dream match for the fans."

Billy's favorite tactic in the ring is the bearhug, for which he is famous. Given his

Superstar Billy Graham vs. Bruno Sammartino (*George Napolitano*)

strength, the hold is a devastating one for his opponent. Lately, fans say, Billy seems to be getting more ruthless in his attempt to regain his belt. In matches against Rhodes, Ivan Putski, and the like he pulls out all stops and charges for his man like a hungry bear.

But Billy is not always the one to deliver the blows. He himself has become bloodied in several matches and has suffered many injuries. "I've never broken a bone, but I received a bad infection in my left knee from mat burn. They had to open my knee up and clear the infection out. It was pretty bad, because it started to spread and could have caused amputation of my leg if it wasn't caught in time."

Billy has on occasion teamed up with his half-brother, Luke, but most people feel that

Superstar Billy Graham vs. Chief Jay Strongbow (*Frank Amato*)

Billy has too much of an ego to compete in anything other than individual competition.

Billy believes he is not so much a vicious wrestler as an exciting one. He cites Ivan Koloff as his choice for the most vicious.

Superstar Graham is not flip about his career. He takes it very seriously. In addition to watching his strict diet and training from two to four hours in the gym every day, he studies matches carefully. "After a match I'll probably be up all night, thinking about the things I should have done or the things I did do and constantly reviewing the match in my mind."

He is also passionately loyal to the sport of professional wrestling. "I don't know if wrestling can be improved," he says. "There are 22,000 people here tonight, sold out, in Madison Square Garden. Probably 10,000 trying to get in. I don't know if you could improve it. The top people have perfected the sport and sold out coliseums all over the world.

"Bruno Sammartino and myself hold the all-time record in the Philadelphia Spectrum for the amount of people ever to be in attendance in that building—19,800 people last Christmas for a match. It's hard to improve on perfection."

Billy is big on absolutes, no doubt about it. And he is an absolute wrestler. One must admire his strength, his stamina, his speed, and his dedication to his sport. And as for his ruthlessness and rulebreaking, he believes that his fans enjoy his style.

"Keep tuned to Superstar Billy Graham," he says, "because I am the most exciting wrestler, the most entertaining, and . . . *I will again wear the belt.*"

Luke Graham

Luke Graham, of the famous Graham family of wrestlers, is more than formidable at 6 feet 3 inches and 291 pounds. He glares at me and demands, "Don't call me Crazy Luke, Crazy Luke. It disturbs me something terrible. I wish everybody would refrain from that." He demonstrates how irritating it is by saying my name over and over, adding "Crazy" in front of it. "If you had ten thousand people out there screaming at you, Crazy Roberta, do you think you could do your job properly?"

One must admit that it is distracting, although Luke seems to have no problems doing his job effectively, if not always "properly." He is an awesome wrestler, a strong wrestler, and one that many opponents dread getting into the ring with.

The nickname Crazy Luke must have come from somewhere. "Well, I do have to admit I deserve it, in the ring, from time to time," he says sheepishly. "It came about that way. And they do it because they want to see me make a mistake. They want to see me get beat. They don't like me. I don't know why. I'm better than anybody else."

Modesty is not one of Luke's finer qualities. In fact, many fans believe that Luke has no finer qualities. His actions in the ring qualify him for that notorious title of rule-breaker.

"I think they wrote the rulebook; so we might as well go out there and break it. If you have the guts to do it." Luke's justification for his sometimes shameful tactics in the ring is that he's "in there to win, and if I have to break the rules to do it, I'll do it."

Anyone who has seen Luke wrestle knows what rules he will break—just about every one. His famous taped thumb (with who knows what underneath) has often found its way brutally into an opponent's throat, leaving the man dazed, near choking. Luke Graham doesn't only try to win his matches, he tries to annihilate his opposition.

When asked how he likes to spend his time, he replies, "To have a good time? I wrestle and hurt people."

It is hard to admire this form of wrestling, although one must acknowledge that Luke

Luke Graham vs. S. D. Jones (*Frank Amato*)

Following two pages: Luke Graham vs. Domenic DeNucci (*Frank Amato*)

is strong and fully aware in the ring and seldom gives up an advantage once he has it. But when Graham lifts his beaten opponent up by the hair and, making sure the referee cannot see the foreign object he has in his hand, thrusts something savagely into the near-unconscious man's throat, most wrestling fans are horrified and disgusted.

In one match Luke sent a vicious kick into his opponent's stomach, doubling the man up. He then lifted him up and brought him down, back first, across his outstretched knee, using that spinebreaking move he is so famous for.

But Luke has fought the best and won against the best. He even admits that scientific wrestlers have their place. "It's the basis of wrestling," he agrees. "I think everybody should be a scientific wrestler to a point."

Asking Luke Graham how he got into wrestling, a sport he has been in for 18 years, is perhaps silly. His father was a wrestler, and all his brothers are or were wrestlers. It's the family tradition—the legend of the Golden Grahams.

Many wrestling fans remember the decade from the mid-1950s to the mid-60s when the Graham clan ruled tag team wrestling. In those days Eddie and Dr. Jerry demolished many a man inside that arena. They won the World Tag Team Championship and the United States tag team title. Then Dr. Jerry teamed up with his brother Luke to win the United States tag team belt, and later Eddie, Dr. Jerry, and Luke formed a triple tag team during the mid-1960s.

Luke has won so many titles it is hard for him to recount them all. "I was World Tag Team Champion with my brothers, with Tarzan Tyler [in 1971], Southern Lightweight Champion, Pacific Coast Champion. I could go on and on . . ."

And of course Luke's youngest brother is Superstar Billy Graham, the ex-WWWF Heavyweight Champion. Billy and Luke have recently teamed up and occasionally fight in tag team competition as a ruthless and fearsome duo. They have both been managed by the Grand Wizard of Wrestling, a man not particularly known for his sense of fair play and honest strategy.

Luke lives in Atlanta, Georgia, but travels so much that he gets to spend little time at home. Though not admired by the fans for his tactics, he is nonetheless popular, as one never knows what to expect when watching Luke Graham wrestle. As I sat there talking with him he was chewing tobacco, but all I could envision was him chewing on some hapless opponent's arm.

"My style of wrestling? People would call it sort of unorthodox because they don't know what I'm going to do next. My partners don't know what I'm going to do next. Sometimes I don't know what I'm going to do next. I have quite a repertoire of wrestling holds and moves, and I go for whatever I feel. Sort of . . . emotional."

But even Luke has gotten hurt in the ring. He remembers many injuries, particularly a broken collarbone and dislocated shoulder, but says that he has had no serious back injuries (a frequent problem for wrestlers) because, "I'm an exception among wrestlers. I've got a good back." And people who have seen Luke heave men up onto that back and set them up for his powerful drops would agree with him.

In his spare time Luke is a treasure hunter. "I really like being outdoors and finding treasure." But the other sports he enjoys are not outdoor ones. "I'm an armchair football player. I like to watch football games."

Before a match Luke's opponents are

Luke Graham vs. Larry Zbyszko (*Frank Amato*)

sometimes shaking. But Luke isn't. "I'm very relaxed and everything, but before I go out there I'm keyed up . . . I psych myself up and I'm ready."

There is no question in anyone's mind that Luke wants to be world champion. In fact, the only suggestion he has for improving the sport is to have Luke Graham awarded the belt. He feels his opponents are not really good enough for him because "there's very few in that class."

Who is in his class? "Well, Bruno Sammartino . . . Bob Backlund is in my class . . . just champions . . . and the cream of the crop."

Luke's father, Sonny Graham, was also a famous wrestler, but Luke feels that his brother Dr. Jerry was the one who helped him the most in his career. "He brought me off the farm and put me in a position where I had to compete to get along, and I did."

Luke feels that wrestling is at the top right now and that he belongs at the top of the top. He warns other wrestlers, "Beware of Luke Graham because I'm out to get right to the very top. And whatever I have to do to get there, I'm sorry, but I'm going to have to step on you."

Luke Graham is not a modest man, not always the most decent of sportsmen. But he is sometimes a very honest man. When I asked him who he thought the most vicious wrestler today was, he did not hesitate one second before answering.

"Me," he said, smiling.

Ivan Koloff

Ivan Koloff *is* the Russian Bear. He is 263 pounds of solid strength, frighteningly determined skill, and an extraordinary amount of wrestling speed and knowledge. The fans in Madison Square Garden held their breath for the whole of Koloff's match against Bob Backlund for the WWWF belt in August 1978. They matched each other hold for hold, move for move. Koloff kept coming. Koloff the indestructible. The man that so many wrestlers I spoke to said was the most vicious man in the ring.

Ivan Koloff (*Frank Amato*)

Koloff is also the man Bruno Sammartino praises—while acknowledging his viciousness—as a great wrestler. And Bruno should know. Ivan Koloff was the opponent who did the impossible when he stripped Bruno of his WWWF Championship Belt on the night of January 18, 1971, in Madison Square Garden in a historic match the wrestling world will never forget.

On that night Koloff was in prime form. He had just returned from a world tour and taken Lou Albano, the Captain, as his manager. Albano had bought out his contract for $100,000, believing that the Russian Bear would win the belt.

Even so, wrestling fans felt confident that Bruno would have no trouble with this opponent. After all, hadn't the Living Legend defeated Koloff several times in 1969?

But there was something different about this match. Something they didn't know, something which was only revealed two years later by Sammartino and George "the Animal" Steele. A secret that Lou Albano, unfortunately for Bruno, did know.

The fact was that Bruno had been injured badly by George Steele in a match three nights before his title defense against Koloff. Steele had torn into Bruno's ribs and right shoulder. Steele passed this information along to Albano and the Russian Bear, and they put it to good use that night.

Nothing seemed unusual at the beginning of the match as Sammartino and Koloff charged into the battle. But it was soon obvious that Bruno was not using his two most famous submission holds: his bearhug and his backbreaker. This, of course, was be-

Opposite: Ivan Koloff vs. Bob Backlund (*Frank Amato*)

cause of the injury that had been inflicted by Steele. So Koloff put on the pressure and pounded the wounded ribs of Sammartino. Then Koloff bodyslammed Bruno onto his injured shoulder. Bruno was hurt and stunned, and Koloff saw an easy mark. He delivered his noted Russian kneedrop across Bruno's throat and soon after pinned him for the WWWF title.

Koloff didn't hold the title for long, losing it to Pedro Morales one month later. But his career was made in the wrestling world. He was the grappler from Moscow who had defeated that great Bruno Sammartino, and everyone wanted to see him in the ring. During the next two years he became a popular star in the AWA, where he tried to win the championship from Verne Gagne.

After Sammartino won back his belt in 1973, Ivan tried to take it away from him again on several occasions. He failed. On December 15, 1975, in the very first Steel-Cage Match to be held in New York State, Koloff faced Sammartino once again. And again he failed to win, leaving the cage a bloody, battered, and beaten wrestler.

As mentioned, he challenged Bob Backlund for that belt in August and September of 1978. Many felt that Bob, so much less experienced than Koloff, was doomed. Koloff and Albano felt confident again, especially since Ivan was working on an undefeated record, in matches where he had virtually destroyed his opponents.

Koloff is not known, by the way, for any sense of compassion or sensitivity toward his opponents. He has left many a wrestler unconscious in the ring, needing the aid of a stretcher to get out of it.

In the first match against Backlund, Koloff won because Bob was bleeding too much for the match to continue. But since Koloff could not take the belt away without a pin, a second match was scheduled. This time Koloff became the victim of Backlund's knee-drop and lost his crack at the belt.

Make no mistake: Ivan never quits. Winning that world championship continues to be his goal. "It's the thing that's on my mind at all times," he says. "It has to be."

He feels that his title was stolen from him by Morales and that he has been cheated out of the belt on many occasions. He complains about one recent match against the current champion. "He mysteriously got counted out of the ring. I have a lot of opponents that end up that way for some reason." His sneer signals his sarcasm. He feels that most people are afraid of him.

On that score he is certainly right. He was by far the wrestler most often named by other grapplers as the most vicious, the most brutal man in the ring. How does Koloff feel about having this dubious distinction among his colleagues?

"I'm honored with it," he says, smiling, "because I try to bring myself around to that, if not with words, then with my actions in the ring, because I think psychologically if you can get your opponent to be leery of you you've got the advantage."

Ivan is considered to be one of that tribe termed rulebreakers. "I don't think it's right," he admits, "but if you have to do it to win, then I do it. My objective is to win." But one could argue that Koloff is a different breed from most of the more notorious wrestlers. He never uses foreign objects or steel plates taped to his body; he simply uses his strength and speed and most of all his stamina, that iron quality he projects. He doesn't like grapplers who use artificial devices. "I think that should be stopped, definitely out," he says and cries for better officials and stricter rules. "If the rules were enforced in a stricter way it would make for much better wrestling. I think it should be a contest of two individuals, not who carries the longest blade."

Funny, but he mentions his old "friend" George Steele when asked who *he* considers the most vicious wrestler. "But there's a lot of them," he adds. "Ric Flair is very aggressive, but I don't think he does it because he's vicious. Actually, my feeling is that you go out there and become a little rougher than necessary at times. That goes without saying."

But wrestling fans who have seen Ivan use that kneedrop repeatedly, long after it's necessary to defeat his opponent, or come off the top rope onto the back or neck of a collapsed man, sometimes even when he's lying out of the ring on the concrete, might consider his actions more than just a "little rough."

Ivan Koloff has been wrestling professionally for more than 14 years, all over the United States, in the NWA, AWA, and WWWF areas. His great uncle, Dan Koloff, whom he credits with guiding him the most in the sport, was a popular wrestler in Canada and the United States back in the late 1930s and early 1940s.

Ivan Koloff is a well-conditioned athlete who trains constantly. "I train out with weights every day," he says proudly. "A split routine, six days a week, and I try to run every second day, for three or four miles." The stamina he shows in the ring attests to the effectiveness of his training regimens.

Koloff is definitely a very rough competitor, a driven and ruthless athlete to whom victory is a necessity. He says that his toughest opponents have been Bruno Sammartino and Andre the Giant. "I'd probably put

Ivan Koloff vs. Bob Backlund (*Frank Amato*)

Andre in there because of his size . . . there's not much you can do with that man! But on an equal basis type of contest I definitely would say Sammartino was the roughest."

He explains that he wants to battle with Bruno again soon because he feels that the great grappler is "still in fantastic condition." He also praises the abilities of Superstar Billy Graham. "He's in great shape. He's got more of a bodybuilder's build, but in the ring he can dish it out pretty good."

Koloff admires the abilities of others and says that he feels his list of the best in the sport would include at least 20 or 30 names. Among others, he mentions Mr. Saito, Rick Steamboat, and Billy Robinson.

In addition to the WWWF belt Ivan has collected quite a few titles over the years. He has won the Georgia Tag Team Championship and the Florida Tag Team Championship, the Canadian International Belt and the European Belt. "I still hold the European title," he says.

Koloff excels at many sports, among them tennis, hockey, handball, and golf; and in all

Ivan Koloff vs. Tony Garea (*Frank Amato*)

of them one can assume he is equally competitive. For relaxation he collects antique furniture and coins, but mainly his interests are athletic.

I asked him how he feels before a match, this Russian Bear who always appears to me to be so calm and cruelly confident. "Now I'm quite at ease in the ring because I've been in it quite a while. If it's a large place I may feel nervous, but not nearly as nervous as I used to feel."

Koloff feels that professional wrestling is a great sport. "It's so different from Russia, where I come from, because there it's completely amateur."

He does have a word of criticism for the fans and asks them to stop throwing things into the ring and attacking his car or other personal property. "Use a bit more intelligence when it comes to that," he says firmly.

His severe tone of voice reminds me that I am talking with the Russian Bear, a fearsome man. I ask him what his weight is right now. "Two hundred and fifty-five," he answers.

That is confusing. I thought it was much more. His smile is more than mischievous, slightly malevolent, as he explains, "Oh, that's because of my boots. I wear eight pounds of boots, you know, four pounds a piece. It raises my weight a bit there."

A scene races through my mind: Ivan Koloff goes over to his opponent, who has collapsed onto the hard mat. He looks down and then . . . a kick straight to the midsection! It has happened many times in Koloff's matches. I have seen it.

And now I know that it is eight pounds of red boot that double those men up. I know now why they howl in pain. Ivan Koloff is a determined man. Not a man of mercy at all.

Ernie Ladd

Ernie Ladd is the Big Cat, the self-proclaimed King of Professional Wrestling. He's the Big Cat because he's 6 feet 9 inches tall and weighs 315 pounds, and he's a king because scores of wrestlers have fallen under his blows and his name on the card packs arenas wherever he fights.

He tells you this freely. In fact, he insists on it. He is super-proud and super-strong and fearless. Many fans, however, will hasten to add that he is one of the most vicious rulebreakers in the sport.

"There's no such thing as a rulebreaker," he insists. I want to remind him of his taped thumb, his jabs to the throat, his kicking and pounding tactics. But he clarifies his position: "The only time there's a rulebreaker is when the referee catches you. They don't give you a ticket for speeding, they give you a ticket for getting caught."

Despite his philosophy, Ernie Ladd is popular with wrestling fans and always exciting to watch. This awesome figure of a man has so much speed and strength that occasionally one feels downright pity for his opponents.

His athletic skill, if not his code of ethics, is impressive. Many people in fact remember the name Ernie Ladd from the ranks of the National Football League, where he was a star. He played defensive tackle for the San Diego Chargers, Houston Oilers, and Kansas City Chiefs before abandoning his successful football career to become a major force in professional wrestling.

Ladd still considers himself an all-around athlete. "I'm not a wrestler, I am an athlete, and I play all sports. I'm a football player, a great basketball player, table-tennis player, and I'm also a super wrestler."

As you can see, the Big Cat does not have a low opinion of himself. He goes on: "I'm a chess player, pinochle player, domino player, just about any type of card player. I like indoor games and I like outdoor games."

Ernie often plays games with his opponent in the ring. After one jab from that thumb, his man is usually open to be played with. Ladd picks him up, slams him to the canvas, lifts the slack figure up and drops him again, perhaps delivering a kick or two to the midsection on the way down.

Ernie Ladd (*Frank Amato*)

I asked him why he went into wrestling. "Because I like being a wrestler. It was introduced to me some time ago in California by a guy named Sammy Stan, who took me into training for six months, and then I continued myself. It was very lucrative financially."

Ernie has no problems making money. Wherever he goes the fans are packed in to see the huge grappler, who is one of the largest men in professional wrestling. Ladd holds the North American Heavyweight Championship Belt, which is recognized by many NWA promoters, and twice in 1978 he was the main event on cards held in the Louisiana Superdome in New Orleans, which drew incredible gates.

When Ladd started wrestling, his style was scientific, and many people felt that he was fated to become the greatest of all scientific wrestlers. Now he is hissed at by fans who once admired his astonishing abilities. Why did he change to the more questionable style of wrestling for which he is currently criticized so heavily?

"Because it's indigenous to my personality." I chose not to explore that statement any further. The Big Cat is *mean* in that ring, and he admits it. "My advice to all wrestlers is to stay away from me if they don't want to get hurt. And to the fans . . . when they scream and holler when I'm beating on a wrestler's head, the worse I'm going to be."

Ladd the Giant has had a long standing feud with that other mammoth wrestler, Andre the Giant. These two have fought on several occasions, but Ernie is yet to win a match conclusively against Andre, who is undefeated. Nonetheless he is confident that he will eventually do so. "I'd like to beat Andre on national TV in front of millions and millions of people. I'd beat him one on one.

If it's the right referee, I'd beat him right in the middle of the ring."

Ernie recognizes that he does have tough opponents to fight. "My toughest opponent will always be a champion, because he wouldn't be a champion unless he was a great athlete," he says. He is very candid in his opinions of other wrestlers. "People like Dusty Rhodes . . ." he says, "he can't beat his way out of a paper sack. But take a guy like Ray Kennedy, who is tough, he keeps on fighting, keeps coming all the time. You got a guy like Bruno Sammartino, you've got to break his neck to stop him. He had his neck broken, and that didn't stop him!

"These people are tough opponents," he continues. "You take a guy like Bob Backlund, who never had anything, and he's hungry as a wolf . . . you've got to beat him. Bob's not gonna give in, that's what makes him a great champion."

Actually Ernie did recently fight Backlund for the belt, and though he had a tremendous height and weight advantage over his opponent, he was lifted high in the air and felled by Backlund's famous atomic knee-drop.

Which didn't surprise Ernie that much. He explains, "Size is not the thing that counts as a professional wrestler . . . it's leverage. In fact, it's not the size of the dog but the size of the bite that's in the dog that counts."

Ladd doesn't have any favorite holds in the ring. "I use any hold I can beat a man with," he states, and people who've watched Ernie grapple know that he often uses holds that appear nowhere in the rulebook.

Ernie says he'd choose Superstar Billy Graham for a tag team partner if he was given the option. But most people would agree that a man with the Big Cat's strong

Opposite: Ernie Ladd vs. Dusty Rhodes (*Frank Amato*)

Ernie Ladd vs. Andre the Giant (*Frank Amato*)

sense of identity would prefer to meet his competition alone, face to face, blow for bloody blow.

Ernie Ladd does think a lot of some people. For instance, he boasts about his family. He has four children, three boys aged 15, 8, and 5, and a girl, who is 6. He says that his eldest son is very interested in sports and tells me that he would prefer that he not play football but rather become a wrestler.

Though Ernie admits to being "really edgy" before a big match, he also says that he feels good. "I feel that my opponent's more nervous than I am." He's probably right, for his opponent knows he's going to face all 6 foot 9 of the Big Cat in that ring.

Ernie Ladd, the self-proclaimed King of Professional Wrestling, loves his sport and is obviously very successful at it. But he does think it can be improved in one major way. "I should beat every champion there is and take *all* the belts. And believe me, Ernie Ladd, the King of the Squared Circle—all the belts belong to him."

High Chief Peter Maivia

The brave and powerful Samoan High Chief Peter Maivia had proved himself on the mat for more than 14 years. In India, Hong Kong, Australia, New Zealand, Italy, England, the United States, in fact, in arenas all over the world he had captivated the crowds with his outstanding abilities and his warm, friendly attitude. His strength and knowledge of wrestling maneuvers were feared by the more notorious grapplers, although he always conducted himself like a true gentleman and athlete both inside the ring and out.

Late in the summer of 1978 he surprised the wrestling world by joining up with his friend WWWF Heavyweight Champion Bob Backlund for tag team competition. Backlund said that Maivia had always been a help and a teacher to him and that he felt privileged to fight with him. With Maivia's skill and stamina and Backlund's speed and strength, they were an unbeatable team, and they remained undefeated after scores of tough bouts.

Many fans believed that they could easily take the WWWF Tag Team Championship, thus making Backlund the first man to hold both top belts and putting Maivia in the number-one position, where he belonged. Their manager, the great Arnold Skaaland, was immensely proud of his new team and predicted an unbroken record of triumph over any and all opponents. Maivia, Backlund, and Skaaland were good friends, and they respected one another's abilities. The perfect team, so it seemed, especially when it included a wrestler with the experience and talent of the Samoan High Chief.

What happened on October 21, 1978, in a televised match held in a Philadelphia arena will never be forgotten by wrestling fans. It was called by some one of the worst atrocities ever in professional wrestling. And Peter Maivia was responsible for it all.

The match in question pitted Maivia and Backlund against Spiros Arion and Victor Rivera, two noted rulebreakers in the sport, hated by many for their brutality and vicious tactics. From the start it was obvious that something was wrong. Maivia was arguing with Skaaland, his manager. He went in the ring reluctantly and fought for several minutes—impressively, one should add—and then tagged Backlund. Bob was equally im-

High Chief Peter Maivia (*World Wide Wrestling Federation*)

pressive, until he was suddenly felled by one of his opponent's blows. After several minutes of being worked over by Arion and Rivera, Bob tagged Maivia, who stayed in for just a few seconds and then tagged the weakened Backlund, forcing him to go back into the ring, though he had obviously not yet regained his strength from the previous beating.

Backlund was torn into again. Bodyslam after bodyslam, kick after kick left Bob a battered opponent. Finally, he managed to tag Maivia, practically dragging himself across the ring to do it, whereupon Maivia again fought for a few seconds and then threw Backlund back into the hot seat by a tag. With Bob looking as though he was about to collapse, Skaaland and Maivia began a heated argument. All of a sudden Backlund was thrown out of the ring onto the concrete floor, and Maivia attacked Skaaland! The Chief continued to strike his manager, now crumpled in a corner. Bob Backlund, seeing the horror, crawled back into the ring and tried to help his manager. Maivia then turned on Backlund—and held him for punches while Rivera and Arion did their dirty work!

Maivia was finally restrained by Tony Garea and Larry Zbyszko, who rushed in from ringside to help and then carried the wounded Skaaland out of the ring. Backlund was dazed and violently angry. He had been betrayed in the worst way.

And when Peter Maivia, on September 23, 1978, pulled the same stunt on his tag team partner and friend, Chief Jay Strongbow, the fans who had followed him loyally all through the years were more than angry, more than hurt, and definitely felt betrayed.

Why did he do it? How could he turn on his friends in such a cruel way? I left it to the High Chief to answer that question himself, though I already knew that the rather shady tactics of Fred Blassie, manager of rulebreakers, had something to do with it.

"Well, the thing was that all this time I had been a good guy," he explained, "always smiling to people and always happy-go-lucky, but then I suddenly realized that Skaaland and Strongbow and Backlund, they were just using me for their own benefit, for their own achievement."

What about Blassie? "Freddie Blassie got to me for some reason and convinced me that these guys were just using me for a steppingstone. So I decided it was better to break away from it."

Blassie says he understands it better. He claims that money was what he used to "get" to Peter Maivia.

The fact still remains that Peter had been a fan favorite, that millions of people had respected him. "I don't have much to say to the fans now," he said, bowing his head slightly. "Right now I'm not worrying what they think of me. I'm doing what I think is best, and I suddenly realized that this is more important than just being a nice guy."

Whatever can be said about Maivia's actions, his abilities in the ring haven't diminished. The Samoan people awarded him two titles, Chief and High Talking Chief, both great honors, and the wrestling world has similarly honored him with many titles. He has been the United States Heavyweight Champion and the champion in England, New Zealand, and Hawaii, to name just a few of the belts he has held.

Besides his strength and wrestling knowledge, the 270-pound grappler is noted for his ritualistic tattoos, which cover an area that extends from his upper calf to his lower chest, and which are a great source of pride to him. They were put on his body in a special ceremony when he became a chief of

Opposite: High Chief Peter Maivia vs. Superstar Billy Graham *(Frank Amato)*

High Chief Peter Maivia vs. Superstar Billy Graham (*Frank Amato*)

his people. To many he was also considered a High Chief on the mat.

"I learned my profession in Europe," he told me. "I wrestled the best in Europe. I defeated some of them and lost to some of them. But I always psych myself up to be as good as I can be." Peter explained that he started wrestling in the South Pacific, and then continued in New Zealand, where he went to school.

Peter Maivia has always been regarded as a brave grappler, not easily stopped, and he has the scars to prove it. "I've had a broken arm, a dislocated shoulder, an arm pulled out from its socket, and my face is all scarred," he says quietly.

He still has statements to make about rule-breakers, a clan he once abhorred but which, fans now feel, he has joined. He disagrees. "I think George Steele and Butcher Vachon are probably the most vicious wrestlers in the ring. I must say, I don't consider myself a bad guy. I just do what I have to do."

He says that although he doesn't picture himself as a world champion, that is the dream and goal of every professional wrestler, without exception. "But I only go into that ring and do whatever I do and don't worry about becoming a champion." He adds, "Whoever I'm going to wrestle, I am going to do my best to beat him."

It looks as though High Chief Peter Maivia has traveled a long way from his origins in the tropical paradise of the Pacific Ocean. And a great way from the hearts of his fans. But that may not be the case forever. The Maivia strength is there, the skill is there; those nerve holds and leglocks and armbars that no one can apply in quite the same way still attest to his skill as a professional wrestler.

And his sense of sportsmanship? He is still a fair man, to some degree. I saw a glimpse of that fine athlete once during our talk, when I asked him who he thought was the best wrestler around today.

He sat for a minute and then shook his

High Chief Peter Maivia vs. Butcher Vachon (*Frank Amato*)

head slightly, smiling almost in regret. "I must say," he began slowly, "that Bob Backlund, even though he is inexperienced . . . well, he has a lot of strength, and he's young . . . and after all, the best is a world's champion. . . ."

Perhaps he was going to continue, but I stopped him. He had stopped glaring at me now, and his face was softer, the words were less harsh. But I didn't need to hear any more. It was best to let Peter Maivia wrestle with his own conscience alone.

Mil Mascaras

He is a man with a thousand masks. A famous movie star in his native Mexico. A wrestler who never ceases to amaze the crowds with his wide variety of holds and maneuvers. Next to Andre the Giant he is probably the most widely publicized and best loved man in the sport. His fans reside in the United States, Europe, Mexico, Guatemala, Ecuador, Peru, Colombia, Venezuela—all over the world, in fact. Of course the man being referred to is Mil Mascaras, one of the greatest and cleanest of all scientific wrestlers.

Mil Mascaras (*Frank Amato*)

Mascaras is known for his sporting integrity and his skill, which is so vast it intimidates even the most knowledgeable of opponents. And because his physique is amazingly muscular and he is a fanatic trainer, his stamina in the ring is legendary.

His elaborate and colorful costuming is as varied as his holds. His mask, which he never removes (even when acting in motion pictures), changes almost every night. But he can always be identified by his power, grace, and confidence on the mat.

Mascaras has met the toughest opponents in professional wrestling and has handled them with ease. Superstar Billy Graham, Ken Patera, Ernie Ladd, Ivan Koloff, and the Sheik have all at some time or another met their match in Mil Mascaras.

Mascaras is a very confident wrestler, and that is part of his secret. "I don't get nervous," he says. "I don't really worry about the matches because I train so hard every day." He actually spends four hours a day working out at the gym. People in the wrestling world say they've never seen him worn down or out of shape.

Mascaras, with his high sense of ethics, has often become disgusted with his opponents. Or with himself, because of a mistake he might have made. He is very meticulous in the ring, a true perfectionist.

One of his trainers dubbed him the Superman of the Mat because of his high-flying maneuvers; in fact, he is recognized as the best flying wrestler in the sport. In his favorite move, the flying leap, he hits the turnbuckle, comes off it, turns his body sideways, and leaps onto his opponent.

For 18 years the 240-pound grappler from

Mexico City has been amazing and captivating the crowds. He has held the IWA Championship Belt, an honor he is very proud of.

Mil Mascaras, whose name means "a thousand masks," hides his true identity behind that covering. He is allegedly from a well-to-do Mexican family and has two brothers who are also masked wrestlers—El Sicodelico and Dos Caras, with whom he has fought in tag team matches.

A law was passed in New York City several years ago so that Mil could wrestle in Madison Square Garden. There had been a ban on masked wrestlers for over 15 years, but the pressure from the fans who wanted to see Mascaras prompted the change of this law.

Mil was interested in wrestling as a teenager. He trained vigorously to build up the physique that today holds so many in awe. In high school and college he played football, but it was wrestling he decided to pursue. As an amateur wrestler he went undefeated and soon won the adoration of fans in Mexico. While he was training for the Olympics in 1960 a promoter in Mexico City introduced him to the pro mats.

Promoters convinced the flying masked man to come to Los Angeles, and he soon began to build up a following on the West Coast, winning major titles in no time at all. He held the Americas Heavyweight Championship and the Americas Tag Team Championship and fought such grapplers as Fred Blassie, John Tolos, and Ernie Ladd.

There are few areas of the country in which Mascaras is a stranger. In Texas he again had the fans cheering. He held the Texas Tag Team Championship with his good friend, Jose Lothario. He also lost in two tries at the NWA title, against Dory Funk, Jr., and Jack Brisco.

But in his attempts to win the NWA, AWA, and WWWF belts Mascaras never let the fans down; he was always a hair's breadth away from the belt, and quirks of fate were all that kept him from it. In fact he would still consider trying for a belt if given the opportunity, and many say that it's only a matter of time before he possesses one of the three major titles.

In Japan Mascaras is certainly a main event. Only Andre the Giant is cheered as enthusiastically. His skill, speed, and colorful manner delight Japanese crowds just as they endear him to fans in the United States.

In addition to his aerial maneuvers Mascaras is known for his devastating abdominal stretch, which, even when applied to a huge man like Ernie Ladd, usually results in his opponent's submission.

Mascaras has teamed up with some of the best. In Mexico his tag team partner is often Tenables, a famous grappler around those parts, or El Fonto, who is "*the* most famous." In the United States he's been on teams with Pepper Gomez, Chavo Guerrero, Rian Mendoza, Bob Backlund, Pedro Morales, Johnny Valentine, and Jose Lothario.

Mascaras's movie career has been as successful as his wrestling career. He has appeared in 11 films thus far. "They're distributed in the United States through Columbia Pictures," he tells me and explains that he always wears his mask in them and always wrestles. "They're similar to the old-fashioned serials, where the heroine is in trouble, and I'm the hero who rides a motorcycle or whatever and chases the bad guys." Actually, I found out that there were three *big* box-office stars in Mexico—Fonto, the Blue Demon, and Mascaras.

Mil stresses the fact that he takes his sport very seriously, and anyone can see the evidence of that on the mat. He has mentioned that he feels "a lot of wrestlers could use

Following two pages: Mil Mascaras vs. Ken Patera (*Frank Amato*)

Mil Mascaras vs. Ken Patera (*Frank Amato*)

more training as far as their ability in the ring" and emphasizes the need for constant workouts. He is undoubtedly referring to the breed of grapplers who feel they must use illegal tactics to compensate for their lack of skill—a breed that Mascaras has always fought against, both in principle and in action.

Mil enjoys training and weightlifting more than anything else, for his main love is physical conditioning. He also jogs quite a bit. But he has other hobbies as well. "I'm interested in antique furniture," he tells me, "and I collect hand-carved figures in ivory and jade."

Mascaras is exceedingly popular, and he receives letters from all over the world; people ask him how they can become a wrestler like him. He answers most of these letters and is known for always being helpful to his devoted fans.

He expresses his appreciation to all his fans and wants to tell them to continue to support wrestling. One thing is for sure—they will never cease to support him. For when the Man of a Thousand Masks comes flying off that top rope, there is no doubt in anyone's mind that one of the greatest of all grapplers is in the ring—the wrestler *extraordinaire* they call Mil Mascaras.

Gorilla Monsoon

It would be unthinkable to omit Gorilla Monsoon from any book that purports to cover professional wrestling. For over 18 years, in places all over the world, the mammoth size, cool aplomb, and surprising speed of this 6 foot 7 inch, 401 pound grappler has thrilled the crowds that pack arenas to watch him wrestle.

He has had immortal battles with Bruno Sammartino, whom he still names as his toughest opponent. "I still remember those battles," he muses. "I still feel them too when the weather's not too hot; all those old injuries really give me a headache."

In Japan, where they like their wrestlers big, Monsoon was a fan favorite. He was big enough to engage in sumo wrestling several times when he was on tour there.

His wrestling skills have always been solid and varied. Fans know him for his crushing bearhugs, backbreakers, Boston crabs, giant splashes, and sleeper holds, all of which he uses most effectively. For such a big man he moves around the ring with amazing speed, and of course his awesome size makes him a difficult man to pin.

He comes from Rochester, New York, and started wrestling when he was eight years old. "I started in the YMCA systems," he tells me. "I wrestled all through high school and college. I went to Russia, Turkey, Bulgaria, and quite a few Iron Curtain countries with the Olympic team in 1959. Then I was approached by promoters and turned professional."

Today as in the past, Gorilla Monsoon only grapples with the best. He names Bob Backlund, Bruno Sammartino, Dusty Rhodes, Billy Graham, Nick Bockwinkle, and Jack Brisco as men he considers greats on the mat. He fears no opponent and never has.

"I have an open contract on promoters' desks all over the country that anyone can sign. There's only a handful of us that will do that. It really doesn't matter to me who I wrestle. I'm at the point in my career where I know enough about this sport that no one can really go out and do a super number on me and eliminate me. I have the ability to protect myself in there, I know what my capabilities are, and not too many men can honestly say they know their capabilities."

Monsoon does have amazing abilities. In

Gorilla Monsoon (*Frank Amato*)

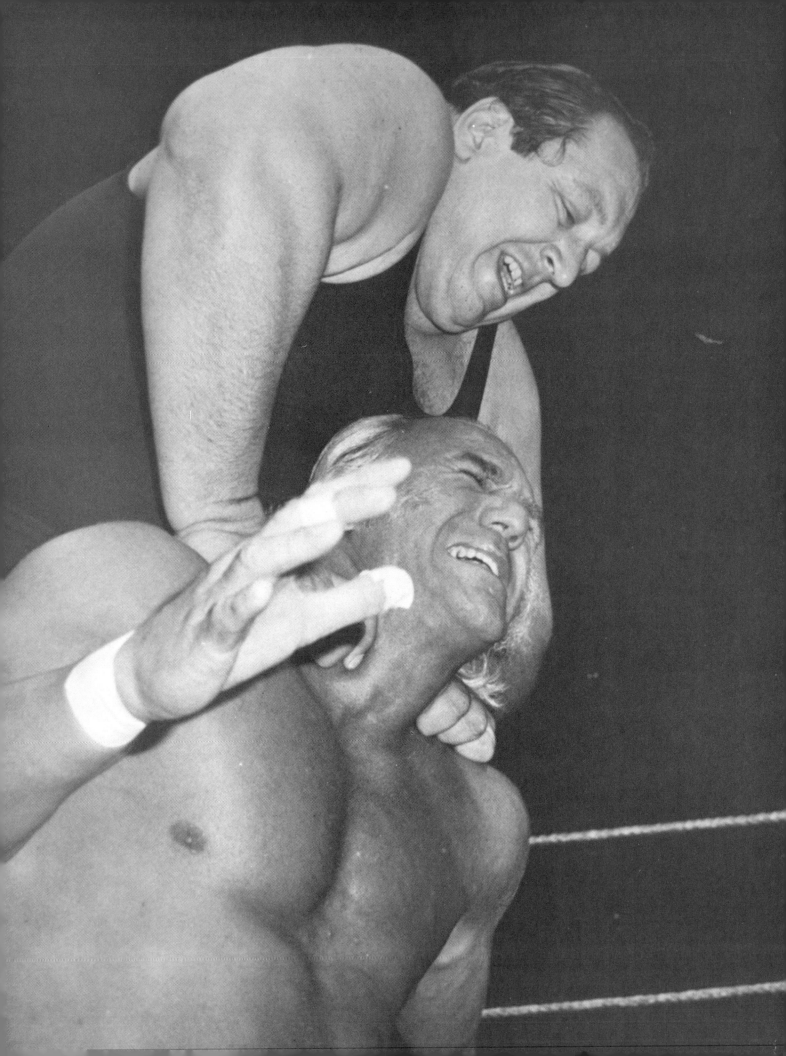

addition to being a skillful and strong wrestler, he is an extremely intelligent, open, and confident man. He believes wrestling could be improved in one major way—the dissemination of more information about the wrestlers themselves to the fans. He is adamant on this point: "Fans have very little insight as to what is really going on and what professional wrestling is about," he begins. "What are some of the sidelines of these men? What do they earn? What do they do when you don't see them inside of that squared circle? I think something should be done along those lines. I think that wrestling fans are the most loyal and greatest fans in the world, and they're entitled to know something more about their favorites.

"The wrestlers are not just 250-pound cauliflower-eared, musclebound refugees from a gymnasium. That's not the case anymore. Twenty years ago that might have been true, but today 85 percent of the men in this sport are college graduates and have many sidelines that are unique and interesting."

I couldn't have agreed with him more. I had found wrestlers to be fascinating, articulate individuals who had far more to offer than just their mat skills. I explained to Gorilla Monsoon that this project was about just that: telling the fans more about wrestlers and wrestling.

I asked him about his hobbies and interests and, as in many other cases, found them to be numerous and varied. "I play racquetball, I bowl, I play pool. I like to travel and see parts of the United States I haven't seen. I like to listen to good classical music, and spend as much time with my family as I possibly can."

Monsoon has a wife and three children, two daughters, 18 and 13, and a son, 15. He says proudly that his son is an all-round athlete.

Gorilla Monsoon, who is fundamentally a great sportsman, had some interesting observations to make about rulebreaking in the sport. He first told me that many state athletic commissions impose fines on wrestlers when they break rules, following the advice of the referees. "Rulebreaking in this sport can cost you a great deal of money." And he is not opposed to the fines; to the contrary, he feels there should be more of them and that they should be higher.

He went on to explain how he interprets rulebreaking. "There are many underlying reasons why gentlemen break rules in this sport. I think that's part of the box office. There's more excitement in hockey when they drop their gloves on the ice than there is when they score a goal . . . that's what people are looking for today. They're looking to be entertained, and they're looking for excitement. Automobile racing draws a great deal of spectators because people are, in my opinion, basically sadistic."

Though an uncomfortable thought, I had to admit that there was a lot of truth in it.

Gorilla Monsoon is as fearless in the ring as he is vocal about what he does and doesn't like. He is noted for his cool both before and during a match; the way he drops and pins opponents with studied ease. But as he remembers the injuries he received from Sammartino he recalls the other mishaps he suffered as well. "I've broken all my ribs more than once," he begins, embarking on an incredible catalog of injuries. "I've had the cartilage removed in one knee, I've broken both ankles, had a countless number of contusions and concussions. Several vertebrae in my neck have been moved around, three quarters of the

Opposite: Gorilla Monsoon vs. Superstar Billy Graham (*Frank Amato*)

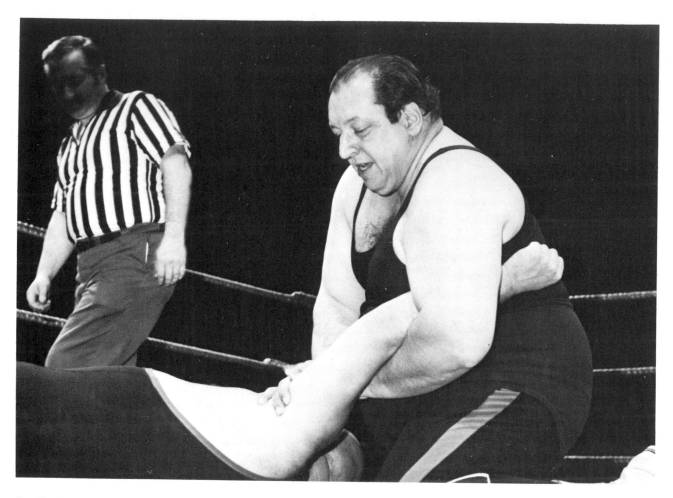

Gorilla Monsoon vs. Butcher Vachon (*Frank Amato*)

way." He laughs. "Other than that, nothing serious."

But he goes on to discuss what he means by the last flip statement, and it explains a lot to me about the endurance of the grappling greats. "You know, as professional wrestlers we learn to live with a lot of injuries that would put the layman home in bed. We're in there with broken ribs and dislocated shoulders and sprained ankles . . . you just learn to live with those things."

It's the dedication to the sport and to the fans that he is talking about when he explains the pain-tolerance levels of wrestlers. "If you're in the main event in Madison Square Garden, well, 21,000 people don't want to hear you've got a sprained ankle. They want to see you."

Gorilla Monsoon is not the kind of man or wrestler who would let down the people who are loyal to him. He has proven that in many ways, over many years, in the squared circle and intends to keep on doing so for a good many years to come.

Ken Patera

Wrestlers sometimes have nightmares about a maneuver called the swinging neckbreaker. Some claim that it is potentially fatal. The man who uses it, who has mastered it, and who has applied it mercilessly on several occasions is a man who himself describes his style as "brutal at times." He is the 275-pound Olympic Strongman, the medalist from Portland, Oregon, the man who went from a shining light to become one of the most feared and villainous types ever to walk into the arena—Ken Patera.

Once considered a brilliant scientific wrestler and the strongest man in the sport, Patera, led by his manager, Captain Lou Albano, decided to choose the path of active rulebreaking. He now insists that he is only after money in the ring and will use any means he can to get it. In addition to his intimidating strength, he uses several deadly speed maneuvers and still retains a vast amount of wrestling knowledge and skill. In short, he is one of the most fearsome wrestlers in the world.

Patera was temporarily banned from wrestling in the WWWF region shortly after his "incident" with Billy White Wolf. At the time White Wolf was Jay Strongbow's tag team partner, and they held the championship. In a match against White Wolf, Ken did the usual—he clamped on that swinging neckbreaker, and though his opponent submitted, he refused to let go, causing extensive damage to White Wolf's neck and back. White Wolf was hospitalized, and though the Indian tried to make a comeback in Hawaii, he was just not strong enough and had to be hospitalized again.

Patera has hospitalized three other wrestlers besides White Wolf—Kevin Sullivan, Johnny Rivera, and Juan Lopez, all young men on their way up. They all fell victim to the neckbreaker, which Patera will not release until he feels his opponent has been demolished.

Patera, who is the current Mid-Atlantic champion, says he became a wrestler because of the traveling involved. "I've always traveled," he explains. "I've been all over the world as an amateur shotputter and weightlifter. I've been on international teams for

Ken Patera vs. Mil Mascaras (*Frank Amato*)

over eight years, and I saw in pro wrestling a way to keep traveling. The competition also appeals to me . . . and it's money, really. Actually, I got to the top very early in my career. The money is quite lucrative . . . I've been up to around $100,000 a year."

When Ken attended Brigham Young University, he was a shotputter and a discus thrower as well as a weightlifter. In 1968 he went to the Pan American games, stymied the opposition, and won the meet. He did the same in 1969, 1970, and 1971. Then came the big chance for which he had built up his body and trained for all those years: the summer Olympics of 1972, held in Munich, Germany. Ken Patera represented the United States there in weightlifting. Though he didn't win the gold medal, he did win the bronze medal and so went down in Olympic history.

On his return to the United States he was besieged with offers, many to join pro football. But he turned them down and selected a career in wrestling, putting himself under the guidance of Verne Gagne, who then held the AWA Heavyweight Championship.

Patera proved to be an apt pupil. He started his pro mat career in the AWA and showed he could handle the best, winning many more bouts than he lost. He fought such opponents as Nick Bockwinkle, Baron von Raschke, Ray Stevens, and Blackjack Lanza.

Then Patera went to Texas to get more experience—and gained a hated rival in the form of Superstar Billy Graham. The feud still simmers, and Patera says that although Graham claims he is the strongest wrestler, that is nowhere near the truth; Patera feels he, himself, is the strongest and that the man second in strength to him is Bruno Sammartino.

Ken returned to the AWA and pleaded for a chance to fight for the belt. It never came, nor did the bout he wanted with NWA champion Terry Funk, and so, bitter, he turned to Lou Albano, who convinced him to give up his scientific style for that brutal style we now expect of this Olympic strongman.

With Albano by his side, Patera wrestled in the Southern area of the country, now breaking the rules. He soon became the Brass Knuckles Champion in the Oklahoma-Louisiana territory. He then went on to the WWWF region, fully transformed with his rough new image. His hair went from brown to blond, his manner went from quiet and humble to loud and boastful. And he began to apply that swinging neckbreaker for longer and longer periods of time.

Ken describes this change from another viewpoint: "When I came out of the Olympic Games, I was All-American, the Olympic champion, winner of medals. By the way, I still hold all the American records for weightlifting," he says in an aside, then continues, "Anyway, I presented myself as the people's choice, more or less. Because of my aggressiveness, however, I felt a lot more at ease being aggressive. Even as an amateur, I spoke my mind. If I didn't like something, I said it. I just carried this over into wrestling. That's why I feel I'm such a success right now, because I do what I feel I have to do in the ring."

Ken still considers his style scientific because he is not lackadaisical, trains every day, and knows a great deal about wrestling skills. And it is certainly true that even in recent scientific matches with people like Bob Backlund, he has been able to match the best of them hold for hold.

Speaking of his most famous hold, Ken explains that the neckbreaker is nothing more than a full nelson with his own tremendous strength behind it .

Opposite: Ken Patera vs. Mil Mascaras (*Frank Amato*)

Ken Patera vs. Ivan Putski (*Frank Amato*)

Patera says he feels a lot of tension before his bigger matches, mainly because of his competitiveness. "You want to go out there and win," he says. "You don't want the other guy to completely dominate you, you want to completely dominate him."

And dominate Patera does. He gives his opponents nightmares. He knows it, and he is proud of his abilities. He considers himself to be intensely individual and doesn't like to fight in tag teams. "In tag teams you have to rely on your partner. I wrestle 90 percent of the time on an individual basis. I've never really gone in for team sports."

When asked his opinion of other top wrestlers, he praises the abilities of Ric Flair, Greg Valentine, and John Stud, men with philosophies similar to his. He also praises the fans, as long as they show him respect. "But if they knock me down and degrade me, well . . ." He frowns, and his face becomes hard and steely. "As long as people pay me respect, I'll pay the same back. As of late, I haven't had much respect . . ."

I decided at that point, for my own good, not to explain to Ken Patera why he isn't getting what he wants from his fans. Some things really are better left unsaid . . .

Ivan Putski

There are some professional wrestlers who have tremendous skill, the kind of strength and stamina that is awesome. There are others who hold the complete attention of the crowds from start to finish, who are loved by their fans with an incredible ferocity. Ivan Putski is lucky enough to fit into both these categories.

When Putski enters the ring, you know by the shouts and cheers that everyone in that arena is behind him. "I'm popular because I'm Polish," he says with a smile. But every wrestling fan knows that understatement for what it is. Putski has the fans' attention because of his skill and most of all, his strength, which is legendary. His 5 foot 10 inch body is 240 pounds of solid muscle, a physique he keeps in shape and is very proud of.

"Training is like eating to me," he says. "If I don't train I don't feel right. This is my profession, my body, it is my life, so I must stay in good shape."

Men like Superstar Graham, Ivan Koloff, Bobby Duncum, and Ernie Ladd, to name just a few, could attest to that strength, as they have often found themselves on the receiving end of it. Though Putski says he considers them tough opponents, you know that the Polish Power always has things under control in his bouts with them. "I like the headlock," he says, referring to his favorite hold, "because if I applied it with all my power and strength, I could break a guy's neck. I can do that, you know. It's subtle, but it's also like a vise."

Even so, Putski rarely resorts to vicious maneuvers unless he has no choice. In fact, he often loses his temper when his opponents break the rules: "If you break the rules, I break the rules too. Even Steven. That's my game. I don't like rulebreakers."

Putski comes from Krakow, Poland, the original home of the Pope, John Paul II. "I'm real proud of that," he says with a smile; he is proud of his heritage and his people.

Ivan Putski saw his country taken over by Communism. The wrestler Danny Pleaches discovered Putski in Poland and brought him to the United States. He began his professional sports career in football, as a fullback for the Detroit Lions. Then he injured his knee and had to quit. As he enjoyed con-

Ivan Putski (*Frank Amato*)

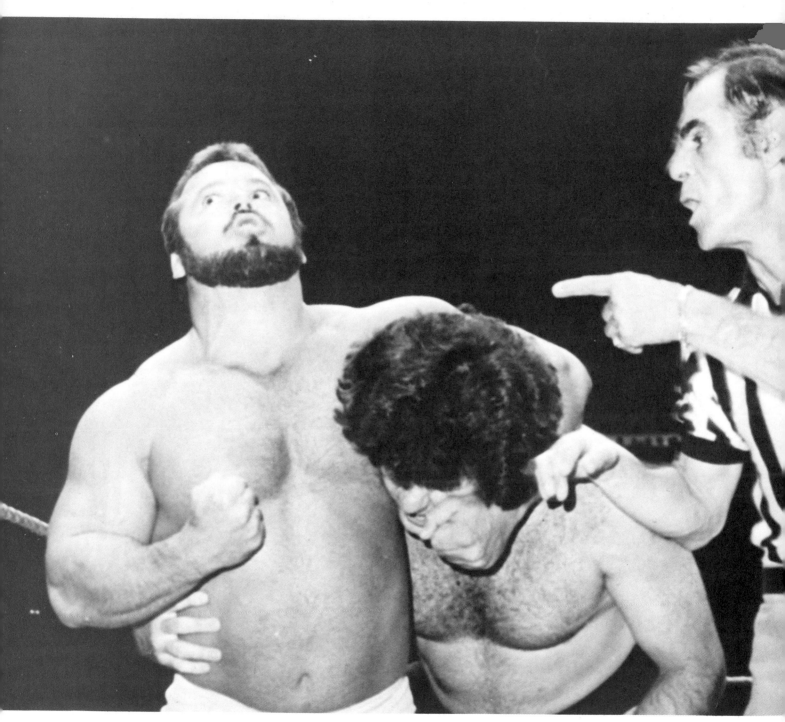

Ivan Putski vs. Spiros Arion (*Frank Amato*)

tact sports, namely boxing and wrestling, the mat world was a logical choice for him.

Ivan has held a wide variety of titles. The American Heavyweight Belt, the United States Heavyweight Championship Belt, and the Texas Belt have all been his. Before venturing into the WWWF territory he enjoyed great success in Texas, Minnesota, Wisconsin, Louisiana, Oklahoma, and Europe, where he went through all his matches with ease.

The list of brutal opponents Ivan has faced is amazing; it includes just about every fearsome grappler one could imagine. One of his biggest feuds was with Stan Hansen, the man who seriously injured Ivan's friend Bruno Sammartino. In fact, while Sammartino was recovering from that injury in the hospital Putski wrestled Hansen in a bloody bout to even the score.

Putski considers Ivan Koloff the most vicious wrestler, and because of their differing political and athletic ideologies their bouts have been filled with blood and determination.

Though Ivan considers himself the best wrestler around, he would pick Dino Bravo (and has picked him) as a tag team partner: "He's a good man, and I know I can rely on people like that."

Ivan's interests outside the ring include raising plants. Just as he is serious about his sporting skills, he is dedicated to his hobbies. He raises unusual tropical plants in a formal greenhouse.

I asked him how he felt before a match, being a man who shows nothing but bravery once inside the ring. "I used to feel nervous when I first started," he admits, "but after ten years, well, I can get my teeth knocked out, nose broken, leg broken, it's just one of those things I expect, and I try not to think about it. And I try not to be nervous."

Besides his strength and bravery, perhaps one of the best explanations for why Ivan Putski is so loved by his fans is because he loves them back. "I always take fan mail and say hello to a fan or sign an autograph no matter where I am, a restaurant or wherever . . . whereas a lot of wrestlers, the guys who are stars, won't do it. But to me, without the fans the sport would be nothing.

"I love people, you know. I love to mingle with people, and I just love my fans."

It is generally said that only a truly strong man can afford to reach out and be open. Ivan Putski is such a man, and the same kind of athlete. He has that kind of "power."

Ivan Putski vs. Baron von Raschke (*Frank Amato*)

Harley Race

Harley Race won the NWA championship belt from Terry Funk on February 6, 1977, in Toronto, Canada. Race first won this title when he defeated Dory Funk, Jr., in May 1973, but lost it on July 20, 1973, to Jack Brisco in Texas.

When Race won the belt from Terry Funk, many people in wrestling smirked, believing that he could not hold on to it for long. That was a serious error, for Harley Race proved himself night after night, facing all contenders and sometimes fighting every day in the week.

Harley Race (*Frank Amato*)

Race has a peculiar blend of nastiness and rulebreaking on the one hand, and skill and consideration on the other. He has gone to great lengths to make sure all worthy wrestlers have the opportunity to fight him, yet he can pull some underhanded tricks once in the ring. But despite his violence and the rage he sometimes exhibits, he has a high regard for his opponents' abilities. He is out not to maim his foes but rather to win against them by employing any means he can.

The 248-pound grappler from Kansas City, Missouri, is no stranger to the mat world. He had been wrestling for over 19 years and has been interested in the sport since he was a small boy. "Gus Karras, from St. Joe, Missouri, started me out in wrestling," he says. "I used to go to matches at night and beg Mr. Karras to let me wrestle and to train me. After a while he did."

When Harley Race first won the NWA belt from Dory Funk, Jr., it was the culmination of nearly 15 years of mat wars. In the beginning Race had one close friend in professional wrestling in the person of Larry Hennig. Once these two men ruled the AWA areas as the World Tag Team Champions. They held this title for over two years. Hennig remembers that even in those early years Race was possessed with a driving ambition to wear the belt.

When Race lost the NWA title he had so craved to Jack Brisco, he was tormented; all he could think of was getting that belt back around his waist. There wasn't a match he'd turn down. Along the road back Race wrestled the very best. He won many matches

Harley Race vs. Rocky Johnson (*Frank Amato*)

and many impressive titles: the Florida state title, Southern Heavyweight Championship, and the Missouri state title, twice.

He tried to win back the NWA belt from Brisco but failed. When Jack Brisco lost it to Terry Funk, Race hoped his luck would change. Eventually it did: He regained the belt, injuring Terry Funk with his Indian Deathlock hold.

After regaining the NWA belt he faced such opponents as Dick Murdoch, Dusty Rhodes (a true rival and top contender), Rocky Johnson, Ox Baker, Ric Flair, Jack Brisco, Mr. Wrestling II, Wahoo McDaniel, and Chavo Guerrero; the list is very long. Race does not shy away from any man who desires to fight him and has the background to do it.

When you watch Race in the ring, you realize immediately that he is all business. He has one thought in mind: to win the match in the quickest way possible. He is an excellent wrestler and can match holds with the best. Though he can get rough in the ring and is not above kicking or punching, he is normally not overly vicious.

Harley Race vs. Jack Brisco (*Frank Amato*)

THE STARS

One of his pet maneuvers is diving off the turnbuckle in a deadman's drive, head first, butting into his opponent as he lies on the mat. This is devastating considering Harley Race's size. Race is also adept at using a suplex and has won many matches with it. And his skill with the piledriver (a dangerous maneuver where the wrestler takes his opponent's head between his knees, then comes down backwards into a sitting position, driving his opponent's head into the mat) is widely known and feared.

Race tells me that he considers Andre the Giant one of his toughest opponents, which is no surprise, since most other grapplers I'd spoken to said the same thing. Race says he feels "kind of tense" before a match and "very relieved" after it.

In his spare time Harley plays tennis and golf, skis, water skis, and scuba dives. He also enjoys being with his family, though with his fighting schedule he has little time for anything else. He detailed his schedule for the next few weeks for me: He was off to New Zealand for one day, back to the States that night to fight, off to Charlotte on Tuesday, to Miami on Wednesday, Norfolk, Virginia, on Thursday, St. Louis on Friday,

and St. Petersburg, Florida, on Saturday. Harley Race is indeed a fighting champion.

Because of his insane schedule he doesn't have to train very much anymore. "I used to lift weights and work out all the time," he explains, "but now I wrestle every night. That's my workout."

Harley Race is dedicated to his sport and works very hard in the ring. He takes his work seriously, as anyone who has watched him fight can see. He would like wrestling to receive more publicity and would also prefer to see only skillful, properly trained wrestlers in the ring. It is his honest desire to face the best challengers rather than cling to a belt pointlessly, ducking tough matches, that makes him a great wrestler and a good sportsman, whatever might be said about his roughness and occasionally brutal maneuvers.

Over the years Harley Race has made his mark in professional wrestling, and that mark, though somewhat tainted, is one he should be reasonably proud of. He has worked hard for his position at the top and has earned the respect of many for his skill. People no longer smirk when Harley Race steps into the ring.

Dusty Rhodes

For one of the few times during the match the crowd was silent. Superstar Billy Graham had collapsed outside the ring, fallen onto his knees, blood flowing from his head and running in streams over his chest. He looked dazed and defeated. Suddenly his opponent reached down and pulled him back into the ring by the rope that linked the two by the wrists. On the rope was a metal cowbell, and it was in the hand of Billy's opponent. It came crashing down on Billy's head, and the crowd went wild. With horror? Never! Graham's opponent could do no wrong. He was the prince of the ring, the king of the fans' favorites—the American Dream, Dusty Rhodes.

Many people connected with professional

Dusty Rhodes (*Frank Amato*)

wrestling could convincingly argue that Dusty Rhodes is the most popular grappler in the arena. The crowds love him for his hard tactics, his flamboyant style. Dusty, in his sequined cowboy pants and studded hat, is a sight not to be missed. And when Dusty downs another challenger and climbs onto those ropes to throw kisses out to the crowd, the roar is deafening.

Dusty Rhodes fights all over the country and challenges only the best of opponents. He has fought Harley Race for the NWA belt several times and has come breathtakingly close to winning it. He has had bounties placed on his head by wrestlers like Race and the Funks, has brutally and effectively settled feuds with grapplers like the Masked Assassin, and has held the Southern Heavyweight Championship of the NWA longer than any other man.

Dusty Rhodes's career in professional wrestling would take a book to detail. His popularity speaks for itself—just as Dusty speaks for himself. He is no more at a loss for words than he is at a loss for quick action when his opponent is charging. He is the master of bloody, dangerous matches like the Texas Bull-Rope Match, and he fears no one. He is, in his own words, "an outlaw."

The 265 pound grappler from Austin, Texas, comes from very humble beginnings. "I was the son of a plumber and got my first paycheck when I was 8 years old, digging ditches," he tells me. "I wanted to be a superstar, an entertainer. I wanted to move masses of people." Certainly the Dream got his dream.

"I have a great following of people. You

Opposite: Dusty Rhodes vs. Spiros Arion (*Frank Amato*)

know I grew up with Mexican-Americans and black people where the whites were a minority. So everything I'm talking about I've done. They did repossess my daddy's TV. I'm real, and the fans can identify with it." Dusty insists that the fans can sense his sincerity. "I think they can see through you if you're a phoney. They work all week, they pay money to see me. If they bring four kids, maybe fifty, sixty dollars, and if I don't give them what I say I'm going to give them, I rip them off, and they can see a rip-off."

Dusty is a cool character, a jet-setter now, who speaks with a fast, Texas accent. His energy seems always to be at a peak level. He tells me that yesterday he flew his 308th flight that year, and that this was more traveling than anyone else in wrestling did, Andre the Giant and Harley Race included.

Dusty's dream is to wear that WWWF belt, something he has always wanted. He objects to being denied it when the champ is a scientific wrestler; he feels that anyone should be given the chance to fight for it—and that he especially deserves a shot at it. He thinks that his challenge for the belt would be "the greatest gate attraction in the history of wrestling." He has no intention of keeping quiet about his demands either. "They can't shut me up and say don't do it. They're not going to 'cause I'm an outlaw to the extent where no one has ever been able to tell me where to go or how to be."

Dusty is a fearless wrestler. While I was talking to him I couldn't help noticing the layers of scars that creased his forehead. "Well, you see my injuries," he said, pointing to his head. "I had 360 stitches there, I've had injuries in my knees, my ribs, I hurt all the time, but it's part of me because I like what I'm doing."

Dusty freely admits that besides the physi-cal activity and the roar of the crowds, the dirt-poor boy from Texas in him also loves the money he makes in professional wrestling. "I'm into silver screens and limousines," he says with a smile. "When I go to New York, I drive around, and I'm as big as any rock star. I go to Gucci's, and when you're from Austin, Texas, and your dad's a plumber, well . . . my dad would have no idea what a 'Gucci' was. . . . I drive myself hard to be successful, and I make more money now than I'd ever thought I'd make in my life."

Dusty is a hard player as well as a hard worker. He has a taste for clothes—as is evident to anyone who's seen him in the ring—and a taste for horses. But the thing he enjoys the most out of the arena is music, country and Western, rock, you name it. Music is an integral part of Dusty Rhodes's life. Recently he even cut his own record, and listeners say that he has a fine singing voice.

Dusty Rhodes vs. Superstar Billy Graham (*Frank Amato*)

THE STARS

"I guess a lot of my philosophy comes from Bob Dylan's stuff and Willie Nelson's stuff, because I grew up with Willie in Austin. When I was 15 years old, he used to play around the clubs, and people used to sneak a six-pack of beer out to us in the back, where we listened to him. I'm really into music." Other favorites he mentions are Kenny Loggins and Donna Summer, and he prides himself on being part of the "in" crowd of Andy Warhol and the Rolling Stones.

Dusty's favorites in the ring include Bruno Sammartino ("A great man, a legend"), Billy Graham ("He's strong, he's powerful, he's colorful, he sells tickets"), Dory Funk, Jr. ("He won the NWA championship for five years, and to watch him, I don't think anyone could touch him skillwise—the greatest wrestler of my era"), and Dino Bravo ("good-looking kid"). He readily admits that he doesn't think he is the most skillful wrestler around, but that doesn't bother him. He believes he is the most popular—"bar none!"

His main complaint in the ring is not about rulebreakers, whom he expects and can handle, but about referees, who he believes should be formally trained in a school. "There's too many old referees," he says. His one other complaint is that he can't get on national television to tell his story the way Muhammad Ali does. "I want to be as big as he is, but they won't give me the national time I believe is coming to me now. I want to sit down on TV in my Levis and have five minutes to talk about myself as a human being for the millions of fans who want to become personally involved with me, who want to know what I'm like."

Dusty Rhodes is electric to watch in the ring. He gives the fans, as he says, "120 per-

Dusty Rhodes vs. Eric of the Yukon Lumberjacks
(Frank Amato)

cent," and his popularity backs up that claim. He is as exciting to speak to as he is to watch, and yes, I do believe he is sincere. Dusty is dedicated to his sport and to giving his fans the best he has.

"I'm sincere about my business, my talent, about where I want to be," he insists. "The main thing is that I like what I'm doing. My dad always said that was the main thing. He used to get up at five-thirty in the morning to go be a plumber, but he loved doing it, he believed he was the best of plumbers."

With a philosophy like that, the American Dream is unbeatable.

Victor Rivera

Back in May 1975 Victor Rivera won the WWWF Tag Team Championship with Domenic DeNucci as his partner. To everyone's surprise Rivera relinquished his half of that crown only one month later, and DeNucci was left to find a new partner, Pat Barrett. But that was not the only surprise Victor Rivera had in store for the wrestling world.

In those days, Rivera was considered a very formidable scientific grappler, tough and skillful. The popular Puerto Rican was never at a loss when it came to handling an opponent, and he always did it fairly and squarely.

Then, upon his return east in 1978, he joined forces with manager Fred Blassie, known for changing the minds—and tactics—of many scientific wrestlers, and Rivera became a rulebreaker. Fans were aghast as they saw Rivera's knee smash down repeatedly into the chest of his semiconscious opponents; saw him apply choke holds, pull hair, jump on men who had fallen out of the ring, and attack seriously wounded opponents needlessly.

His only justification for his actions was the chase after money and the championship belt. He explains, "In the beginning I was a scientific wrestler, but I was interested to see if they could give me a better opportunity to wrestle the World Heavyweight Champion. And I talked to Fred Blassie. He manages me now." I asked him if he felt that by using more aggressive tactics he would have a better chance of winning that coveted belt. "Correct," he stated firmly.

The 253-pound grappler has been a professional wrestler for over 12 years. His in-

terest in the mat world began early, when he had just come to New York as a child and watched wrestling on television. "I enjoyed it on TV," he says, "so in the YMCA I started lifting weights, doing gymnastics, and then a friend of mine started to teach me how to wrestle. By the time I turned 17 I was a professional."

Rivera has traveled to arenas all over the country and the world. Whatever his tactics may be, he is a great success, and fans are fascinated with his speed and awesome powers.

"A lot of people boo me, and a lot of peo-

Victor Rivera (*Frank Amato*)

Victor Rivera vs. S. D. Jones *(George Napolitano)*

ple discuss the way I am wrestling now, but that's my bread and butter," he says. "And I have to go all the way to the top, defeat my opponents and become the champion. That's the only way."

He is single-minded in his determination to wear the belt. He says he has no favorite holds or maneuvers. "When I go in the ring, my intention is to win, no matter how. I use anything, and any tactic that will make my opponent suffer and give up."

Rivera mentions Spiros Arion, a frequent tag team partner, as a great wrestler, along with Ray Stevens, Luke Graham, and Superstar Billy Graham. Interestingly enough, he says that George Steele is "very vicious in the ring." Many fans would say the same about Rivera!

Victor mainly enjoys training and working out when he is not in the ring. He also enjoys spending time with his wife and two children. He tells me that his nine-year-old son is showing the same early interest in wrestling that he did.

There is no escaping the fact that Rivera is a talented and tough opponent who is widely feared and never taken for granted. He is also a man who loves the sport he is a part of, and he would like to see more young people become involved in sports in general and wrestling in particular.

"I'm happy the way I am," he says, "and I'm happy in my profession. I make a lot of money. And I hope that a lot of young souls will come along and do the same; don't stay in the street, come into this profession. Any sport, I believe, is good."

Bruno Sammartino

We were sitting there, talking about this book, on the night of his comeback in Madison Square Garden, October 23, 1978. It occurred to me that I was sitting with a man who was a legend. And I also knew that I sat with someone with such style, such command, such inner as well as outer strength that I could do little more than listen in admiration and awe.

I sat that night with Bruno Sammartino, the living legend of professional wrestling. The man who held the WWWF Heavyweight Championship for a total of more than 11 years. The man whose neck was broken by Stan Hansen and who still came back, against all odds, to excel once again in his sport. The man who had just this night triumphed over the wrestler who had taken his belt, Superstar Billy Graham, with amazing ease.

To write about Bruno's career in full would take another book. And perhaps such a book should be written, for no one has meant more to or done more for professional wrestling than Bruno Sammartino, from Abruzzi, Italy.

"Not too long ago," he begins, "I really thought of retiring. Not because I felt I couldn't produce anymore, but just because I thought, Maybe it's time. I made some sort of announcement to people on radio and television. And I was flabbergasted, really, by the reaction it got. I have gotten so much mail saying, 'Don't quit . . . we like you, we think you're the greatest . . . ,' and I'll tell you something, when you get that kind of reaction from a fan, boy, you just get revitalized all over again."

Bruno has always been a fan favorite, and he has always cared deeply for his fans. Fittingly, his first return to the WWWF after over a year's absence was for charity, at a match held in Asbury Park, New Jersey, for the National Juvenile Diabetes Foundation. The match was against the Iron Greek, Spiros Arion, a grappler known for easily demolishing his opponents. But the Sammartino strength and wrestling knowledge were too much for the rulebreaker; with a sensational combination of armbars, leg-

Bruno Sammartino (*Frank Amato*)

locks, lateral hammerlocks, and other great fighting maneuvers Bruno chalked up yet another victory.

Before that people had wondered if he had gotten soft, if he was too old, too tired. At Asbury Park, as in the Garden, he showed them all that Bruno Sammartino was not a thing of the past.

"I had the title for over eleven years," he tells me when asked whether he wants to regain his belt, "and it was fantastic in a million and one ways, but I think enough is enough. I just want to enjoy wrestling where and whenever I feel like it and not have the obligation of any title."

Bruno Sammartino first won the WWWF Heavyweight Championship from Buddy Rogers on May 17, 1963, in an incredible 48 seconds. After losing the title to Ivan Koloff in 1971, he regained it from Stan Stasiak in 1973. He finally lost it to Superstar Billy Graham in Baltimore on April 30, 1977, in a still disputed match, where Billy used the ropes for support in pinning Bruno.

The roster of grapplers Bruno has taken on reads like a who's who of professional wrestling: Mr. Fuji, Koloff, Graham, Stasiak, Baron von Raschke, Harley Race, Bulldog Brower, Baba, Professor Tanaka, Pedro Morales—the list is endless. He avoids no opponent.

"My favorite opponent is one I feel can go out there, whether he's rough or not, but has the skills to enable me to show my skills. . . . I don't care how rough he is."

Bruno is a completely scientific wrestler, though he can be a very tough fighter when he needs to be. In fact, he spent some time as a boxer and even went five rounds with Sonny Liston. He surprised me with this when he explained how he originally got into wrestling.

"I come from a small village in the moun-tains of Italy. We had a guy there that had represented us in the Olympics, a Greco-Roman wrestler. And he liked kids. He was just a nice guy, and he had a little mat in his basement. He used to like to teach kids and work out with kids. And I got interested im-mediately, the first time I ever went on a mat.

"When I came to this country and was wrestling as an amateur, I had a light-heavyweight champion by the name of Al Quale—he was a darn good fighter. And he tried to change me from wrestling into box-ing, and I did it for about six, seven months. My heart was never in it. It brought me here to New York. I fought Sonny Liston for five rounds. I fought people like Billy Johnson, who used to be a sparring partner for Floyd Patterson. But it just wasn't my thing. I never felt as comfortable as I did on the mat."

Wrestling has changed to some degree over the many years of Bruno's career, but his feeling for it has not. He is obviously proud of what he does and good at what he does. Recently, he has also added to profes-sional wrestling by doing ringside commen-tary with Vince McMahon, Jr., in WWWF area matches.

"I would like to see more wrestlers try to show their talents in the ring," he says. "To try to impress the fans through their skills and abilities rather than gimmicks, because it's these gimmicks that have brought more and more controversy into my profession, which I've never liked, was never happy about.

"I didn't like it then, and I don't like it today, and I still hope that not only the wres-tlers but the promoters as well would do away with that kind of nonsense and show the people that they are well-conditioned athletes who can compete in a tough sport and don't need that kind of buffoonery to stand out in the eyes of the fans."

All pictures in color section by Frank Amato

Bob Backlund

Bob Backlund vs. Spiros Arion

Bob Backlund vs. Superstar Billy Graham

Bob Backlund vs. Ken Patera

Dino Bravo vs. Eric of the Yukon Lumberjacks

Haystacks Calhoun

Tony Garea vs. Superstar Billy Graham

Opposite: Superstar Billy Graham vs.
Chief Jay Strongbow

Ivan Koloff with Captain Lou Albano

High Chief Peter Maivia vs. Superstar Billy Graham

High Chief Peter Maivia vs. Ken Patera

Mil Mascaras vs. Superstar Billy Graham

Ken Patera vs. Tony Garea

Ivan Putski vs. Baron von Raschke

Ken Patera vs. Ivan Putski

Opposite: Ken Patera vs. Bob Backlund

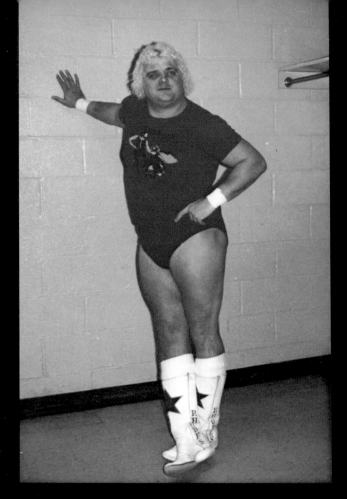

Dusty Rhodes

Bruno Sammartino vs. Stan Hansen

Bruno Sammartino vs. Ken Patera

Stan Stasiak vs. Mil Mascaras

Baron Mikel Scicluna vs. Stan Stasiak

Chief Jay Strongbow

Chief Jay Strongbow vs. Professor Toru Tanaka

Mil Mascaras vs. Superstar Billy Graham

High Chief Peter Maivia

Dusty Rhodes

Superstar Billy Graham vs. Ivan Putski

Bruno Sammartino vs. Ken Patera

Superstar Billy Graham vs. Bob Backlund in a Steel-Cage Match

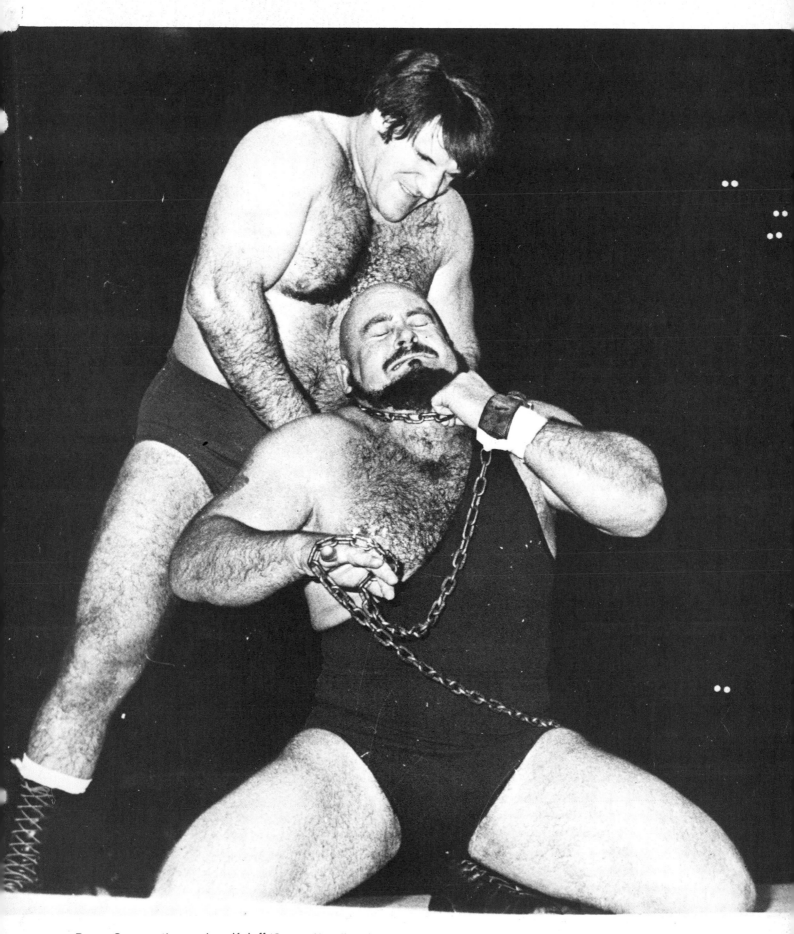

Bruno Sammartino vs. Ivan Koloff (*George Napolitano*)

Bruno believes that it's not the vicious rulebreakers that bring in fans but shows of true wrestling skill. "All I've ever worn at this is a pair of boots and tights, and I've been received well not only in this country but anywhere in the world that I've been. So I think me and many others like me have been the proof that people just want to see guys who can really wrestle in that ring."

Bruno is a well-conditioned athlete who enjoys fair competition. But he has respect for ability even in rulebreakers. One of the most aggressive wrestlers, Ivan Koloff, once defeated him, and yet Bruno still considers Koloff a great athlete. "In Ivan Koloff I think you have a tremendous athlete, although people say he's rough. But this is a guy who can be as rough and tough as any other wrestler in the world, but besides that he knows all the other wrestling skills. He's got tremendous stamina."

So Bruno's one criterion for what makes a great wrestler is ability. He is a true competitor, a true sportsman, in that he respects his opponent's talents regardless of his feelings about the man. "To me, if you have great stamina and strength, I say that you're a worthy foe."

Bruno Sammartino has proven time and time again that he is unbeatable, even when everyone else believed he was defeated—as they did when his neck was broken and he was told by two doctors he would never be able to wrestle again.

"One of the top neurosurgeons in the country and the orthopedic surgeon who handles both the Steelers and the Pittsburgh Pirates told me I wouldn't be back. As they told me, I came within one millimeter of being paralyzed from the neck down."

Bruno did come back, even though he received many more serious injuries. He once cracked two vertebrae in the small of his back and suffered a slipped disk. But

Bruno Sammartino vs. Stan Stasiak (*Frank Amato*)

THE STARS

Bruno, as one can instantly see, is not a quitter, which perhaps explains his position at the top of the wrestling world for all these years.

Does Bruno worry about being injured again when he goes into the ring? "Well, I've been at this a long time." He smiles. "If you mean by that, how do I feel about getting hurt, or do I think about my previous injuries, or how good a match it will be . . . none of that enters my mind. The only thing that enters my mind is not to disappoint the fans that have paid to see Bruno wrestle."

Sammartino is a confident man, a relaxed man who enjoys his work and his life. At home he is an opera buff. "I have my music room at home, and when I'm relaxing, I go into my room and close the door so I don't disturb anybody else. I play all my operas and my favorite artists.

"*Romeo and Juliet* is a beautiful, beautiful opera," he adds, "but I prefer the Italian. Not to sound prejudiced, but I think the most beautiful operas are in Italian."

That fascinating combination of super-strength with warmth and sensitivity has appealed to millions of wrestling fans through the years. Bruno's skills have also astonished wrestlers, who generally view him with great respect and sometimes abject fear. His style is unique and spontaneous, and his holds and wrestling knowledge are incredibly broad and varied.

"I like to show my speed," he says, commenting on his favorite moves in the ring, "and throw in some quick armdrags or some scoop slaps to see if I can catch him coming off the ropes. Years ago I used to be a back-breaker. I've lifted some pretty heavy men. But since I had that serious back injury in '68, I've avoided stuff like that because I don't feel I have to impress people with strength. I lifted people like Haystacks Cal-

houn, who is over 600 pounds! But now I'd rather display some wrestling or some speed or stamina—those kind of things rather than strength or a particular hold."

The fans, all 22,000 of them that packed the Garden in a record-breaking attendance the night I spoke with Bruno, were obviously glad that Bruno was back. And he was glad to see them supporting him once again. He gave them the best, which is really the only thing he has ever given them.

"I hope that I'm intelligent enough, within myself, that when I feel that I can no longer be the Bruno that people have enjoyed through the years, then no matter what the crowd reaction will be, I think then I will quit."

But for now Sammartino, the living legend of professional wrestling, graces the arena with a strength and skill no one can forget once they have witnessed him fight. He is glad to be back, and we are all glad he is back. For many fans the sport of professional wrestling will always be synonymous with the name of Bruno Sammartino.

Bruno Sammartino vs. Baron von Raschke (*Frank Amato*)

The Sheik

Wrestling's greatest man of mystery, violence, and controversy remains the savage and enigmatic legend, the Sheik. For over 14 years the Sheik has packed arenas with fans who come to jeer and gape at his brutal tactics and horrifying surprises, not to mention his stamina, strength, and considerable wrestling skill.

Many people over the years have called for the Sheik to be banned from the arenas. He has used an arsenal of incredible and terrifying weapons against his opponents, all of which have brought into question the good sense of having healthy men meet up with him: weapons like "the fire," which he has tossed in men's faces, seemingly out of

The Sheik with Abdullah Farouk *(George Napolitano)*

nowhere, to blind them, and his razor-sharp teeth, which have sliced through many a scalp in that ring, to cite two examples of his savagery.

Yet the Sheik is an extremely wealthy man, who owns a mansion in Michigan which looks like Tara looked in *Gone With the Wind,* who has vast holdings in oil and real estate, and whose extensive wardrobe boasts over 100 suits and 30 sports jackets, all custom-made.

The Sheik is known only by that name. He rarely gives out information about himself. Other than that he was born in Lebanon and weighs 250 pounds not much is known about him. Yet he is a celebrity in the Middle East as well as in the United States. He was United States Heavyweight Champion for a number of years, proof that he does possess true skill.

To communicate with the Sheik one must talk to his interpreter, closest friend and manager Abdullah Farouk. Attired in a sequined jacket, green silk scarves with diamond stick pins, and large sunglasses, Farouk is no more forthcoming than his illustrious protégé. But he is more communicative, because the Sheik will not speak English. Many people believe the Sheik can only speak Arabic. "He does speak English," Farouk corrects me. "He doesn't particularly like the English language. He doesn't think that it is really attractive to the ear, and he prefers to speak his native one." So I resigned myself to interviewing Farouk. For whatever reasons, I would be able to do no more than look at the Sheik.

Opposite: The Sheik vs. Pedro Morales *(George Napolitano)*

I asked first about the Sheik's most vicious opponent, knowing that the feud he has had with this grappler is one of the longest, bloodiest, and most vehement rivalries in wrestling history.

Farouk smiled in a mysterious way that hinted at the secret powers from Allah that the Sheik is reputed to possess. "I would say without a doubt that his number-one nemesis in that respect is a gentleman who hails from the sovereign state of Indiana and answers to the name of Dick the Bruiser." I knew that some of the matches between the Sheik and Dick the Bruiser had ended in bloody chaos. After one match, held in Detroit in 1977, the Bruiser and the Sheik continued to assault each other all the way back to their dressing rooms. "It's a matter of two egos clashing," explained Farouk. "The confrontation between the Sheik and the Bruiser is both in and out of the ring."

These days the Sheik fights in the Midwest, headquartering in Detroit and working a great deal in Tennessee, Louisiana, and Los Angeles.

I asked Farouk how the mysterious, mystical Sheik became a wrestler. "He was a wrestler in the old country, and the demand for him spread to this country. I heard about him, and we've been together now going into our fourteenth year."

Farouk explains that the Sheik enjoys wrestling because it is a way of "letting out pent-up emotions." He also enjoys the financial benefits. "If you consider counting money a sport, it is one of the Sheik's favorites and one of mine," Farouk said when asked about the Sheik's outside interests. "The only jogging that he and I like to do is right to the teller at the bank. We try to get the money pretty even on both sides of our hips so it doesn't throw us off stride."

Farouk feels that the only way to improve professional wrestling would be to allow the Sheik to "wrestle twice a day instead of just once a day." And as far as the Sheik is concerned, the best wrestlers consist of a group of one. "He'd tell you the best wrestlers around today," Farouk said, grinning. "Just come to his home and look in the mirror. And you'll see the one and only, the unbeatable man himself, the wild man."

Farouk explains to me that the Sheik is a very complex person, a man endowed with mysterious gifts, and a very ordered individual. He follows a strict routine before every match. "He will not put anything in his stomach after four o'clock in the afternoon. He doesn't believe in eating late. He likes to feel free before the match. He feels he can do his best work on a more or less empty stomach, and he's very much of a dedicated man. He's devoted a great deal of his life to his business, and it shows by his success."

The Sheik is a big drawing attraction, although one could not say he was popular with the fans. In fact, he is so unpopular that they come to jeer him. The Sheik knows this, and he is not too pleased with the situation. Asked how he feels about his fans, Farouk stated flatly, "Very, very bitter." Farouk went on to emphasize the point. "You know there's always some kind of a feeling toward a foreign person, and the . . . fact that he chooses not to speak the English language and speak his Arabic language instead seems to instill some hostility in the fans. That hostility that the fans show toward the Sheik and myself is returned twenty-fold by us. We just don't think any more about them than they think about us. It's a mutual love affair, only it's called hate."

Though Farouk attributes this hatred to the Sheik's foreign birth, most fans would

The Sheik vs. Pedro Morales (*George Napolitano*)

deny that, saying it is because of his cruel and brutal tactics. Either way, the Sheik does not let it affect his style. He goes on wrestling, with success, with a lot of blood, and in total silence.

Stan Stasiak

There is one taped hand in professional wrestling that strikes instant fear into the hearts of opponents. And I don't use the word "hearts" loosely. Because that is where the hand goes for, and when it lands, an adversary can barely breathe, much less fight to avoid a pin. The hand that delivers the famed heart punch belongs, of course, to former WWWF champion Stan "the Man" Stasiak.

On December 1, 1973, Stasiak defeated Pedro Morales in Philadelphia to become the new WWWF Heavyweight Champion. But his reign was short, for nine days later he was defeated in Madison Square Garden by Bruno Sammartino, the first man to win that championship belt twice.

Stan Stasiak vs. Bruno Sammartino (*Frank Amato*)

Since then, Stasiak has met all the top challengers in the country and has rolled up an impressive record of victories, if not so admirable a record in tactics. Managed by the notorious Grand Wizard of Wrestling, this 272-pound grappler is noted for his sometimes excessive cruelty.

During his more than 20 years in the ring he has developed his heart punch into a devastating finishing hold. But fans are starting to notice that the heart punch rarely seems to find its mark. He claims that the first man to learn how to counter it was Tony Garea, but it seems now that many others have learned how to defend themselves against that punch of death.

He tries to explain away its failure. "There comes a time in every athlete's career where his specialty at one time or another suffers a downfall, until he finds a change of pace. This is what I'm doing right now," he says, eyes gleaming. "I'm developing a change of pace with the heart punch. There's no way I'll let it slip, because it has brought me so much success and it's devastating when applied. I have found a formula I can't reveal right now, but the fans and the experts will see for themselves."

So Stan the Man plans to annihilate a new round of opponents and regain that championship belt. "That is something every athlete strives for, to be on top."

Oregon-born Stasiak has always been an athlete, but not always a wrestler. He was once a boxer, and before that, a hockey player. "I played in the Quebec Amateur Hockey Association. This probably accounts for a lot of my aggressiveness."

Stan Stasiak (*Frank Amato*)

His characteristically aggressive style and hot temper are actually what turned him toward pro wrestling in the first place. "On one particular night the last hockey coach I had told me I had so many penalties that it just seemed like there was trouble every time I got on the ice. He said 'You know what you should do—become a professional wrestler, then you can really let all this steam out.' So that's what I did, and that's how all this happened."

Stasiak's coach probably didn't realize at the time that he was directing the young player on a road that would bring him tremendous success, if not necessarily the love of the crowds.

But unlike other wrestlers who are not loved by the fans, Stasiak feels a great deal of loyalty to them. "I think the fans are great," he says. "I would say 99 percent of them are great, nice people."

Stan cites Peter Maivia, Chief Jay Strong-

Stan Stasiak vs. Domenic DeNucci (*Frank Amato*)

bow, Gorilla Monsoon, and Ivan Putski as rough opponents. But above all, his fear and respect go to Bruno Sammartino, the man who defeated him. "Bruno's the type of wrestler that can wrestle scientifically but also can fight someone like me, with the temper I have and the aggressive style I use, at my own game. This man, who is in superb condition and has endurance, strength, everything, he can also attack you as viciously as anybody I've ever met."

Stasiak often fights in tag team matches with rulebreakers like Ken Patera and Spiros Arion and makes the most out of his own and his partner's aggressiveness, as he calls it. Once Stasiak gets the advantage, he clamps his opponent in his iron headlock and takes that taped hand and starts pounding away.

Actually, Stasiak describes his style as "aggressive-scientific." He goes on to explain this. "Nobody can deny the fact that I do a lot of real wrestling in there. My problem is that I lose my temper and get that killer instinct. It was planted in me from a very young age when I was boxing and playing hockey. I always learned to go get 'em. That's what I keep in mind when I hear the roar of the crowds. I can think of just one thing—to win."

When he's not in the ring, Stan Stasiak enjoys fishing, but reading is his main source of relaxation, though he says he also devours reading material aggressively!

Stasiak says that he takes every match very seriously. "I don't care if my opponent has only had two or three matches—there is always the possibility of an upset. I always have some concern or tension, but I believe tension is essential to every athlete to make him conscientious of what he's doing. If you lose tension that means you don't care."

Stasiak claims that although he has lost matches recently, anyone will admit that he is not an easy man to beat. And fans who have seen his charging, punch-up style in the ring would probably agree with him. "My wrestling ability is there and my will to win is there. With my reputation everyone knows what is in store for them if they ever happen to wrestle me."

Wrestling Stan Stasiak is not an easy prospect to face, and Stan doesn't intend to make it any easier on anyone either. Though he insists that he is a different person outside the ring and really has no animosity for anyone, inside the ring he is cruel and fierce. He doesn't really consider himself a villain in competition, although that is the way many people see him. The Stasiak smile, which is really a snarl, appears. "I just consider myself a wrestler who can rise to any occasion."

Rick Steamboat

In one of the shortest spans of time known to professional wrestling, a young man from Honolulu, Hawaii, named Rick Steamboat has gone from a praised rookie to one of the major attractions on any wrestling card and one of the major contenders for the NWA championship. Talking to him, sensing his confidence, ease, and charm, one can see why Rick Steamboat has gone to the top almost overnight.

He is a clean, gifted, scientific wrestler with a solid sense of sporting decency, who can face any challenge and handle the most brutal of opponents. He uses his extensive knowledge of karate (which he still studies) in tandem with his wrestling skills, which makes him an unusually formidable fighter.

Rick Steamboat (*George Napolitano*)

"I try to change my style to compensate for the man I'm wrestling," he tells me. "Like, a year ago I was wrestling Blackjack Mulligan, who's 6 foot 8, 300 pounds, and it wouldn't be the same if I was wrestling Ric Flair"—he almost shudders as he adds—"the hardest person that I've ever had to wrestle with is Ric Flair."

Every wrestling fan knows what he means when he refers to this man, his greatest rival and brutal tormentor. Flair, a man definitely not known for his cleanness and compassion in that ring, has a special spot of hatred in his heart for Steamboat.

"He threw me on the floor," Rick Steamboat recalls painfully of one of several bloody matches he and Flair have recently engaged in, "ground my face on the cement. Then he took my belt and ground it into my face. I've got a discoloration on my face that I've had for a month and a half now. I've also got blurred vision in one eye because of it. We've had a feud for a little over a year and a half in this Mid-Atlantic area."

He explains that one of the reasons for that feud, besides the difference in their wrestling ideologies, is the belt—the United States Heavyweight Championship. "Well, I'm the current champion," he says. "He's been the champion . . . this is something that's been going back and forth between us."

Flair is not the only one of Rick's opponents who seems to have a grudge against him; he also mentions Greg Valentine and Baron von Raschke as particularly vicious opponents. In fact, the ill treatment he received at the hands of the rulebreakers al-

Opposite: Rick Steamboat vs. Bill White (*George Napolitano*)

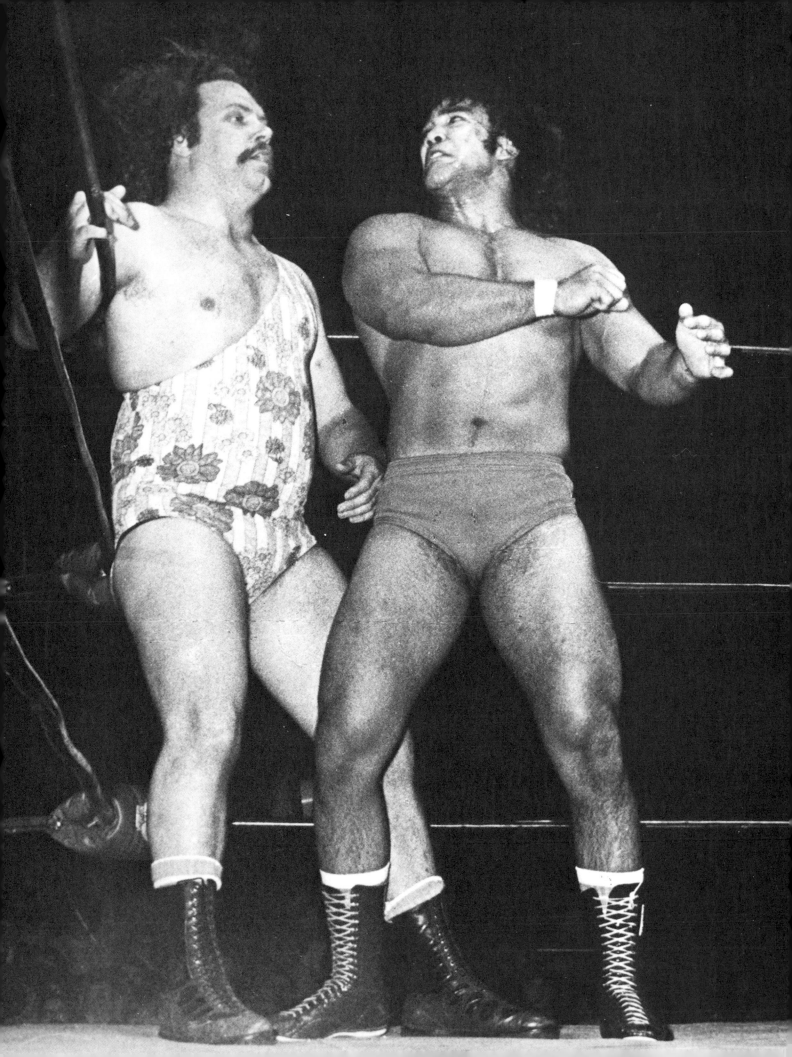

Rick Steamboat (*George Napolitano*)

most convinced him to retire from pro wrestling and only his fans' frantic insistence has kept him in the ring. That and, of course, his love for wrestling.

Rick explains how he first decided on a career in wrestling. "I had an older brother that wrestled seven, eight years ago, who was popular down around Florida and also

THE STARS

this Carolina area. His name was Sam Steamboat. Then I wrestled in high school and college in Florida. It was the best thing I ever did. Of all the sports I ever participated in, like track and football . . . wrestling seemed to be the best thing. It's also been a family thing for a long time."

He goes on to tell me how he got into the professional world. "I was sent up to a camp in Minneapolis. Under the guidance of Verne Gagne and several other wrestlers, I broke in up there at the camp. In every area that I've gone there are a couple of good guys that really helped me out."

Steamboat obviously learned a lot from those days in basic training. The 232-pound, good-looking Hawaiian never ceases to amaze his fans with his versatility. Though his abdominal stretch is one of his most famous moves, he tells me that he hates to rely on just one hold and likes to change them often so that no one will know what to expect from him in the ring. "I've got four or five different holds I use. I come off the top ropes . . . which is legal here. Dive splashes, I do a double chop off the top. I like throwing my opponent in, and I have a move, it's called the double thrust. I have a back-kick and a back-fist. I just don't rely on one particular hold."

In addition to his formal wrestling training, Rick Steamboat has trained for nine years in the martial arts. He currently works on those martial arts skills four or five times a week, in addition to doing weight training to keep that impressive strength of his up.

To relax, he does like to "make the town" after a rugged match and also enjoys working on classic cars, "like older Corvettes." When he has time (which is not often these days, since he wrestles five days a week) he still goes down to Myrtle Beach to hit the surf. Most of the time, though, he is in that ring, either in the Mid-Atlantic area or in Canada.

For a young man, he is very confident and easy when it comes to discussing belts and titles. "Whenever you have a champion," he explains, "they're always made to be beaten. I've been champion, I've lost the belt, I know what it feels like to be on the winning side and the losing side." He tells me that he is happy to be getting such good opponents. "My ability is cut out for me every time I wrestle. In this area the way belts change . . . everybody's ability is so good, you know, it's just like a flip of the coin."

Rick also has nothing but praise for his regular tag team partner, Paul Jones, and also mentions a wrestler from the Fiji Islands, Jimmy Snuka, whom he would also feel proud to team up with.

Steamboat would like to see expanded national television coverage of wrestling; he explains that the televised matches are crucial to the sport, since they "give people a chance to see matches who are perhaps not able to go to the arenas."

Rick Steamboat was named Rookie of the Year by the fans in 1977, and he is now near the top of the list of favorites.

"Without the fans," he says, "there wouldn't be any professional wrestling. I think that their support, personally, behind me, is what has made me, put me where I am."

The fans have done themselves proud in rallying behind Rick Steamboat. A finer athlete, or a more enjoyable person, would be hard to find and many people in the wrestling world point the finger now at Rick Steamboat when asked who will be wrestling's next legend.

Chief Jay Strongbow

The fearless and proud Indian warrior, Jay Strongbow, has been a professional wrestler for 17 years. He is unquestionably one of the fans' favorites and has always ruled at the top of the wrestling world.

With his famous ceremonial headdress (once torn to pieces by two hated rivals, Spiros Arion and Fred Blassie) and his rallying war dances, he always has the crowds on his side, applauding his strength, skill, and his amazing ability to withstand punish-

Chief Jay Strongbow *(Frank Amato)*

ment. His sleeper hold, which almost instantly has his opponents well on their way to dreamland, has won more matches than anyone can count.

Born in Pawhuska, Oklahoma, the Chief is proud of his heritage, proud of his abilities, and proud of his reputation as one of the finest athletes in the world of professional wrestling.

Strongbow may seem to depend a lot on sheer stamina in bouts with his more ruthless opponents, but in fact he is a cautious and thoughtful wrestler. "I regard everybody I get in the ring with as tough. I mean, you can't underestimate anybody. You go in there and you underestimate somebody and you wind up on your back.

"Everybody gives me a good match," he says. "It's hard to say who my favorite is."

However, he does find some opponents more challenging than others, particularly Ivan Koloff. But although he admits to getting butterflies before a tough match, he is always prepared and quite capable of coping with anything that might happen.

"I've tried to create a style that would confuse other people, and it seems like it's worked."

Strongbow first came to the WWWF region in 1971, and in no time became a great hit with the crowds. They admired his pride and stamina, and they began to cheer when Chief Jay Strongbow began to recover his strength after a vicious pummeling by going into his now-famous war dance.

Although many other wrestlers have remained popular with the fans over this long time span, few others have been able to sus-

Opposite: Chief Jay Strongbow vs. Baron Mikel Scicluna *(Frank Amato)*

tain the support of the crowd for as long as the colorful native American.

Strongbow is also popular because of his generous actions. He has unselfishly given much of his time and effort to a number of charitable causes, and he is always ready to speak to admirers or sign autographs.

"If it weren't for the fans, I wouldn't be in a match. If they didn't come to see matches, we wouldn't have wrestling." He doesn't understand wrestlers who say they don't care about their loyal supporters. "It's just like in football, baseball, or hockey, in anything. If the fans are not there, you just don't have hockey."

Over the years, the brave Chief has sus-

tained a host of injuries. Broken ankles, torn-up knees, dislocated shoulders, ribs, wrists, and fingers are all painful memories of Jay's career. But he has always returned to the ring, unafraid, loving the sport of wrestling and the excitement of competition.

Strongbow has held many prestigious titles. "I won attacking championships three times, and I have a lot of individual titles— North American Champion, Southern States Champion, and many other individual state championships."

The Chief started out as an amateur wrestler. "I worked in the farm fields, on a combine, on wheatfields. And a fellow named

Chief Jay Strongbow vs. Superstar Billy Graham (*Frank Amato*)

Don Eagle, who's passed on now, started me in professional wrestling. But I did a lot on my own to get started, too."

Besides wrestling, Strongbow is involved in a great variety of other sports. "I do almost anything. I play golf, racquetball, I bowl . . . I play a lot of things." He also trains constantly. "Practically every day I do something. Running is always good, and weightlifting is good."

Strongbow has a lot of respect for many wrestlers, but says he would prefer working on a tag team with Bruno Sammartino or Bob Backlund. Actually, Backlund's former good friend and tag team partner, Peter Maivia, recently turned on Jay Strongbow in a match they were partners in, just as he had turned on Backlund a week before. Both Backlund and Strongbow were shocked by the violent turnaround in the behavior of their once-respected friend.

Strongbow believes that people may want to see rulebreakers, but that they don't really belong in the squared circle. He has some ideas on how the problem could be curbed.

"Just make stricter rules," he insists. "They can still bend the rules a bit and get away with it. You know, you can't blame the referee—though everyone does—because he's got a hard job. He can't see everything that's happening. Especially in a tag team match, when he's blocked on one side."

But Chief Jay Strongbow is the perfect man to deal with the rulebreakers in the ring. As soon as he applies one of his armlocks, double chops, or especially that sleeper hold, the vicious grappler often begins to come around.

I wind up our conversation by telling the Chief that a friend of mine had seen him fight in Washington many years ago. The match ended when he sustained a severe injury to the forehead—in fact, his head looked as if it had cracked open. He asks if my friend had told me when this happened. I can only tell him that I don't know, but that it got to me, just thinking about it.

"It got to me, too," he says.

The great Indian warrior of the wrestling arena is already a legend, and today he still fights with the same commanding strength he possessed from the very beginning.

Jay Strongbow is an exciting man to watch and a fitting man to admire.

Mr. Wrestling II

The first grappler ever to wear a mask in the ring to conceal his identity was the Masked Wrestler of Paris, in 1873, but the modern tradition of the masked wrestler goes back to the years just after World War II when the sport was first introduced to television. Today, one of the most respected and talented masked wrestlers is the man known only as Mr. Wrestling II.

Mr. Wrestling II is a consummate professional, a methodical, scientific sportsman, a man who rarely loses his temper and relies mainly on his intelligence and superhuman ability to withstand punishment. His code of honor is so strict that he almost retired from wrestling after running amok in the middle of a stormy bout with Abdullah the Butcher. His millions of fans persuaded him to stay

on, but Mr. Wrestling II is still ashamed of the prolonged illegal choke holds he used in that match—no matter how much Abdullah had done to deserve it.

"I don't like rulebreakers," he tells me. "The name of the game is wrestling, and I think all good wrestlers should try to stick to the rules. Pro wrestling is, I feel, the greatest sport in the world."

Mr. Wrestling II has been wrestling since he was 14 years old. He wrestled as an amateur for 10 years, and was later approached by a promoter who suggested he turn professional. But admission into the pro ranks was neither easy nor painless, as he was to discover. "I found out professional wrestling was tougher than I'd ever dreamed." He shakes his head. "I went home many nights with my head hanging between my knees, sore with pain . . . My first few years in the professional ranks I got the living daylights beaten out of me—but nevertheless, that's the way you learn."

Obviously, Mr. Wrestling II has learned. The 232-pound grappler is considered one of the most formidable opponents in the areas where he graces the arena, namely Georgia, Tennessee, Florida, the Carolinas, Alabama, and Louisiana. He is also one of the chief fan favorites, and one of his chief fans is the President's mother, Lillian Carter, who personally invited him to her home. But even for the First Mother, Mr. Wrestling II would not unmask.

"I take great pride in my mask," he says. He refuses to reveal where he comes from or exactly how many years he has been wrestling, but he is more informative about the history of his mask. "I took my name by the

Mr. Wrestling II (*Frank Amato*)

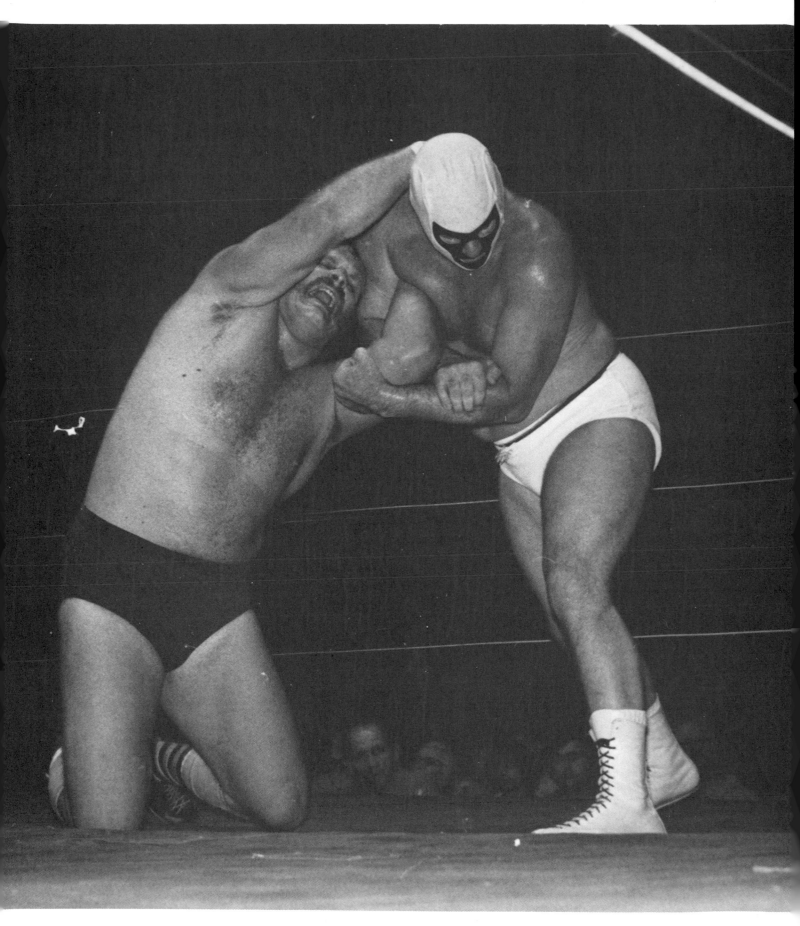

Mr. Wrestling II vs. Ole Anderson (*Frank Amato*)

request of Mr. Wrestling I, Tim Woods. He revealed his identity at a world title match, and so he approached me and asked if I wouldn't mind carrying on the tradition of Mr. Wrestling. Of course, I gave it a lot of thought, because it would mean I would have to keep the mask on at all times and keep my identity hidden, which is not an easy thing to do. But so far I've been very successful with it."

But of course, Mr. Wrestling II depends on more than mystery for his continuing success in the ring. His style is careful and methodical, and he is reluctant to improvise. He has also studied judo, which has provided him with many devastating moves—notably his celebrated headlock, which usually subdues even the roughest opponent.

Another favorite tactic is what he calls the "driving knee." "If I can set my opponent up for it, where I can get him worn down, where he gets up a little off the mat, I back off into left field and I come at him, run him with what they call the big knee. And that's generally where he stays for the count of one-two-three."

Mr. Wrestling's opponents have included some of the toughest in the sport; he mentions four world champions in particular—Harley Race, Jack Brisco, Dory and Terry Funk. For the Most Vicious category he nominates Oly and Gene Anderson, Stan Hansen, and King Kong Mosca, but he has nothing but praise for Bruno Sammartino; his partner, Tim Woods (Mr. Wrestling I);

and younger wrestlers like Tommy Rich. He says that his recent stay in Georgia has been most enjoyable because "all the top competition comes through here."

"I give every match everything I have and don't stop," he says. "As long as I can continue with this attitude, despite any pressure, I think things will go right for me."

Mr. Wrestling II is not only a great wrestler, he is also an all-around sportsman. He boxes, swims, does karate, judo, sumo wrestling, pole vaulting, gymnastics, and track and field, plays tennis, football, baseball, and basketball. In other words, he excels in just about any sport you could name!

He personally attributes his success to the loyalty of his fans, and they clearly mean the world to him. "I love each and every one of them very much. They are the ones who inspire me all the time. I can never thank wrestling fans enough for the support they have given me in the past."

He is proud of his sport and tells me that he has encouraged his sons to become wrestlers. "It earns you respect for your fellow man, and it also teaches you balance, coordination, timing . . . I think it's good for every young boy. It gives him an opportunity to learn what life is all about."

Mr. Wrestling II, though he is totally scientific, admits that if people get too rough with him in the ring, he will be forced to retaliate in kind. And the one thing they must *never* do is pull at his mask! "I warn each and every wrestler—okay, let's wrestle, but lay off the mask. I don't want anyone touching that mask at any time. It infuriates me and I get mad and do things which are not nice."

Well, mask or not, it is easy enough to see beneath the disguise of Mr. Wrestling II. And what lies there? A fine man, an outstanding wrestler, and a contender that has no limit to how far he can go.

Mr. Wrestling II vs. Ole Anderson (*Frank Amato*)

Larry Zbyszko

In 1974 he was named Rookie of the Year in the WWWF region. In 1975 Bruno Sammartino picked him as a future world champion. He has done admirably against such tough contenders as Killer Kowalski, Professor Tanaka, Bobby Duncum, and Baron Mikel Scicluna. And today he is one of the most popular and well respected athletes in the wrestling world.

His name is Larry Zbyszko and there seems little doubt that he will make it right to the top.

"To be a success in what I do," he says, "I put one hundred percent into wrestling. I can't afford to do anything else but wrestle if I'm going into events."

Larry is another of the group of new and upcoming stars who wrestled in college and who take their sport very seriously. He is also a sportsman who brings his share of skill and dignity to the mat world instead of blood and brutality. He's clean and quick, and he has an amazingly extensive knowledge of wrestling holds and maneuvers.

"I just believe in science over brawn," he explains. And watching him fight is testimony enough to that statement. His use of suplexes, backbreakers, and skillful pinning combinations, together with tremendous speed and quick reflexes, show just how good a scientifically trained wrestler can be.

After gaining a solid wrestling background in high school and later at Penn State, Larry Zbyszko began his professional career in 1973 in Pittsburgh, his hometown. And after doing very well in local matches and becoming a favorite in the area, he moved on to bigger opponents and better matches with the likes of Baron Scicluna. He signed with the WWWF a few weeks after Bruno Sammartino regained his heavyweight championship from Stan Stasiak. That time was doubly fulfilling for Larry, as his career has been closely linked with that of the Living Legend.

"I became friends with Bruno a long time ago, and he inspired me. When I was young, I used to watch him on TV and I wanted to be like him. So I tried it out . . . I'm still trying."

Larry Zbyszko (*Frank Amato*)

At 250 pounds, 5 feet 11 inches, Larry bears a striking resemblance to Sammartino in the ring and even uses similar holds and maneuvers. He explains that becoming a successful professional wrestler has always been one of the most important goals in his life—and with the guidance and help of Sammartino, he started out on the right track.

Larry's name has been linked with other famous wrestlers since he joined the federation, namely Haystacks Calhoun and Tony Garea, two men who are favorite tag team partners of his. In both cases the team-ups produced practically unbeatable combinations.

"I can't think of a better partner than Tony Garea," he says. As far as choosing a new tag team partner is concerned, he shakes his head. "I'd just stick with Tony." Garea and Zbyszko won the WWWF Tag Team Championship in December 1978.

But, of course, a grappler of Zbyszko's caliber is mainly interested in individual competition. "Right now, I'd like to wrestle guys like Ivan Koloff, like Bob Backlund in a scientific match . . . any top-name wrestler is who I'd like to be in the ring with."

There is one wrestler Larry doesn't particularly like. "I think the most outright vicious wrestler is George Steele, because he's completely nuts . . . and he doesn't care."

As dedicated as he is to training, Larry does find some time to unwind. "I fly airplanes, Cessnas and Pipers. It gives me a lot of pleasure to go up for an hour in a plane, by myself . . . You're away from everything up there by yourself. It really relaxes me."

He is very serious when it comes to training for a match. "If I wrestle someone I've taken on four or five times in the past, I don't get that feeling of nerves. I know my opponent. I can deal with it. But if I come across somebody who I haven't had the opportunity to watch before, I become very cautious. If he's smaller than me, I can get away with something different. But most men in professional wrestling are a little bit bigger than me, so I have to do different sorts of wrestling and stay away a little bit. Move in, move out, and see what they're going to do."

He explains how he varies his style to fit the opponents. "You can't suplex a 400-pound man like Crusher Blackwell, or someone like Ernie Ladd, who's just so damn tall; if you put him in a backbreaker, his feet are going to touch the ground behind you. On guys who are super big, I stay away from the fancy stuff. With them I'm going to use more basic moves, just pinning combinations and get them tired, on their back, and try to clamp onto them somehow."

Larry makes it clear that he is ready to take on any opponent and that he is aiming for a championship. Many fans believe that it is only a matter of time before he wins a major individual belt.

And the fans are very important to the young grappler. He tells me how much they mean to him, and even apologizes for not being able to communicate with all his fans personally.

"There are a lot of times when I think they get disappointed, because they wait around for an hour or so after the matches trying to get an autograph, and sometimes we don't have the time to stop and sign. I just hope they realize that we might be rushing off to another match. I hope they do understand how much the wrestlers appreciate their patronage, guys like Bruno and myself and Strongbow and Tony Garea and the rest."

It is easy to see that Larry Zbyszko is as decent a man as he is an athlete. We talk

Opposite: Larry Zbyszko vs. Spiros Arion (*Frank Amato*)

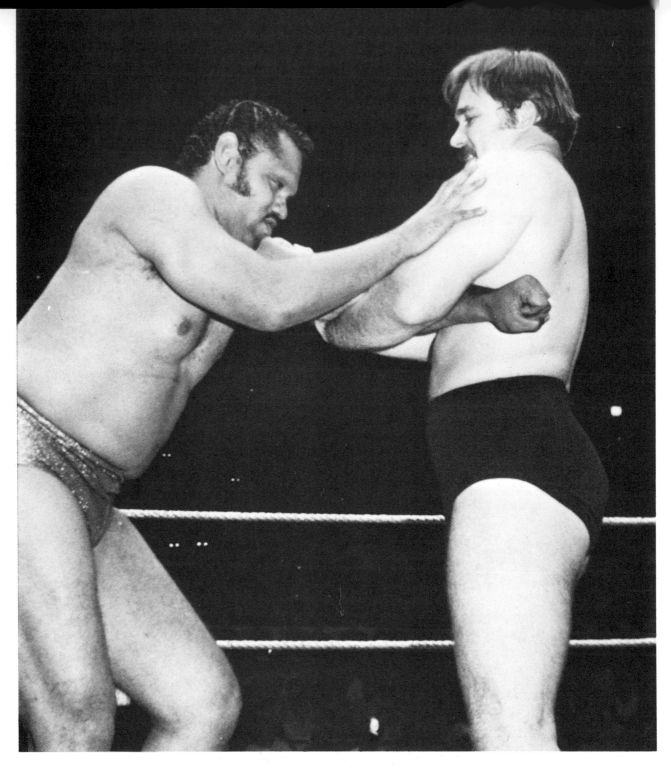

Larry Zbyszko vs. Victor Rivera (*Frank Amato*)

about maneuvers, holds, other wrestlers, and other sports. He is extremely loyal and makes it very clear that he believes strongly in what he does. "This *is* professional wrestling, and I think wrestling is what's going to win in the end."

No doubt there is a young boy somewhere who watches Larry Zbyszko wrestle with the same kind of enthusiasm that Larry had when he sat in front of the TV in Pittsburgh and watched Bruno Sammartino in the ring. If so, then the boy will be extremely lucky if he grows up to be as fine an athlete as Larry is.

★ 3 ★

Tag Team Tandem

Any wrestling fan knows what a tag team is. He also knows that tag team matches are often the most exciting to watch. But to someone not fully acquainted with professional wrestling, the only thing that can be firmly said about a tag team match is that it is a contest with more than one wrestler on each side. Most often, it is a bout between two two-man teams, although there are also three- and four-man teams, and female, and mixed male *and* female, teams as well.

It was in September of 1937 that Morris Sigel, a Houston, Texas, promoter, came up with the idea of putting four men in the ring at the same time. On October 2, 1937, the team of Milo Steinborn and Whiskers Savage faced Tiger Daula and Fazul Mohammed. In those early years this was simply called "team wrestling," because all four men were in the ring at one time. Of course, this situation created problems; four men in the ring meant frequent collisions between teammates and a lot of confusion.

The idea of having one man standing on the apron holding a tag rope and entering only when his partner could tag him originated in Minnesota around 1939. And so tag teams were born, and the idea spread like wildfire throughout the U.S. and Canada in the late 1930s right up to the start of World War II. Girl tag teams developed, like that of

Gladys Gillman and Mae Weston; as did midget teams, noted among them the duo of Sky Low Low and Fuzzy Cupid.

During the war years most wrestling cards consisted of three single matches followed by a tag team match in which four wrestlers who had just fought in the single events participated. This reflected the wartime talent shortage, since so many wrestlers were serving in the military.

During the economic boom of the late '40s and early '50s the sport of professional wrestling thrived, assisted both by stars like Gorgeous George and by new attractions like tag team competition.

Many of those early tag teams were brother or sister combinations. The Crying Greeks (Babe and Chris Zaharias of Cripple Creek, Colorado) were one such team, remembered for their longstanding feud with the Dusek brothers, better known as The Riot Squad.

In 1954 an exciting father and son combination entered the ring in tag team competition, that of Warren and Nick Bockwinkle. Though Warren is now retired, Nick Bockwinkle won the AWA championship belt on November 8, 1975 and is feared and respected by his fellow wrestlers.

One popular tag team in the early postwar years was that of Tarzan (better known now

Stanley ''Killer'' Kowalski (*left*) with his tag team partner, Hans Herman (1951)
(*Courtesy of Global Wrestling Library*)

TAG TEAM TANDEM

as "Killer") Kowalski and Hans Hermann, both huge wrestlers. Kowalski was 280 pounds, 6 foot 7, and Hermann was 6 foot 6 and 270 pounds. They held the World Tag Team Championship for eight months.

Other top teams during the mid-fifties included: Pat O'Connor and Verne Gagne, Buddy Rogers and the Great Scott, Mr. Moto and Great Togo, and Chris and John Tolos.

Tag team wrestling was introduced in Japan in 1953 and is still one of the most popular forms of the sport there today. In fact, two Japanese wrestlers, Mr. Fuji and Professor Tanaka, held the World Wide Wrestling Federation Tag Team Belt three times, first from August 1972 until August 1973, then from October 1973 until December 1973,

and again from September 1977 until they were defeated in March 1978 by Dino Bravo and Domenic DeNucci.

Tag team wrestling was banned in New York State until May 11, 1953; the first match was held in Madison Square Garden that same evening. However, one incident which occurred on November 18, 1957, almost resulted in the whole sport of wrestling being banned from the state. The wrestlers involved were Dick "the Bruiser" Affils and Dr. Jerry Graham against Edouard Carpentier and the late, great Antonino Rocca.

The trouble started when the match was awarded to Rocca and Carpentier. Some of the fans who rushed into the ring to congratulate their heroes started to attack Dick the

The Original Golden Grahams—(*left to right*) Eddie, Dr. Jerry, and Luke Graham (*Courtesy of Global Wrestling Library*)

Bruiser. The Bruiser tried to defend himself by throwing the fans back out of the ring. Rocca and Graham began to tussle and more and more bodies flew through the air. Several fans, as well as policemen, were taken to the hospital as a result of the melee that ensued. The wrestlers were all fined, the Bruiser was barred from wrestling in New York State, and the commissioner warned that if anything of this kind ever happened again, wrestling would be banned altogether in New York State.

The late 1950s saw such tag team greats as the Fabulous Kangaroos. But team action accelerated even more in the 1960s until it became what it is today, an integral and exciting part of any professional wrestling card.

One of the best known brother combinations started in the mid-fifties and continued until 1963. The team was composed of Dr. Jerry Graham and his brother Eddie. They were the only team to hold both the United States Tag Team Title and the World Tag Team Title at the same time. Eddie retired and brother Luke Graham made his tag team debut in 1963. In 1969 the youngest "Golden Graham," Superstar Billy, joined Dr. Jerry as the newest addition to the family tradition of tag team fighting. And of course, Superstar went on to win the WWWF belt from Bruno Sammartino in 1977.

There have been Russian tag teams, Irish teams, Polish teams, vicious teams, scientific teams. There have been so many outstanding tag combinations that it would be impossible to name all, or even a small part, of them.

Some people think that tag team competition is easier than individual competition, since a wrestler who is tiring or in trouble can be relieved by his partner. However, this

Superstar Billy (*left*) and Luke Graham (*Frank Amato*)

also means that tag team wrestlers must know their partners' moves and abilities very well and be able to work as part of a team. Some wrestlers I spoke to told me they would prefer not to fight on tag teams, since they felt that it is in some ways more difficult when you have to watch out both for yourself and another man.

Getting back to history, Harley Race and Larry Hennig were an impressive team combination in the AWA and held the tag team championship a number of times. Race went on to win the NWA Heavyweight Championship on February 6, 1977. Mad Dog and

TAG TEAM TANDEM

Butcher Vachon were also very talented AWA team champions.

In the early 1970s tag team wrestling gained fresh momentum all over the world, and is now mounting to a peak in the United Kingdom. The British Wrestling Alliance even has a mixed (male and female) tag team championship belt.

The '70s have seen some incredible combinations in tag team competition. As mentioned, Professor Tanaka and Mr. Fuji have held the WWWF belt three times; Mr. Sato and Mr. Saito make up another formidable Japanese partnership. Ric Flair and Greg Valentine continue to strike fear and trem-

Mike Graham (*left*) and Steve Keirn (*Frank Amato*)

bling into their opponents; John and Jim Valiant are a very popular brother combination (the Valiant Brothers won the WWWF Tag Team belt in March of 1979); and Steve Keirn and Mike Graham hold one of the United States tag team belts.

Jim Brunzell and Greg Gagne are very talented grapplers, AWA tag team champions, who work together with technical excellence in the ring. Larry Zbyszko and Tony Garea are exceptional partners (and WWWF champions), not to overlook Zbyszko and another partner, 600 pound Haystacks Calhoun.

And no one can overlook the unique eight-man tag team match that was held in Madison Square Garden on January 23, 1978. Captain Bob Backlund (with teammates Tony Garea, Larry Zbyszko, and High Chief Peter Maivia) faced Professor Tanaka, Baron Mikel Scicluna, and Mr. Fuji (Stan Stasiak had been drop kicked out of the ring early in the match). Backlund's team won, but not just because they had the advantage of numbers—after his teammates had been eliminated, Backlund defeated all three opponents singlehandedly.

Speaking of Bob Backlund and Peter Maivia, and how unpredictable tag teams can be, one of the most astonishing outrages in professional wrestling occurred between these two. Backlund and Maivia, long-time friends, teamed up in the fall of 1978 as a tag team combination. Many felt they would be unbeatable together, and that Backlund would be the first man to hold both the WWWF championship and the WWWF tag team championship. But suddenly, in a match against rulebreakers Spiros Arion and Victor Rivera, Maivia turned on Bob Backlund and their manager, Arnold Skaaland, beating up Skaaland and helping Ri-

(*From left to right*) Professor Toru Tanaka, High Chief Peter Maivia,
Baron Mikel Scicluna, and Mr. Fuji (*Frank Amato*)

Mr. Fuji flies off the back of Bob Backlund. (*Frank Amato*)

TAG TEAM TANDEM

Domenic DeNucci (*left*) and Dino Bravo (*Frank Amato*)

vera and Arion beat savagely on his supposed "friend," Bob Backlund. Maivia later explained that he had been brought over to the camp of "rulebreakers" by manager Fred Blassie, known and disliked by many in the wrestling world for his unethical tactics. Backlund is now understandably shaky about wrestling in a tag team. "I feel as though I can no longer trust anyone," he says.

Dino Bravo and Domenic DeNucci had held the WWWF Tag Team Championship earlier that same year, one of the most impressive teams to combine for battle. DeNucci, with his strength and endurance, and Dino Bravo, also very strong and incredibly

Eric (*left*) and Pierre—the Yukon Lumberjacks (*Frank Amato*)

TAG TEAM TANDEM

quick, were like lightning in the ring and it seemed like they could hold onto that belt forever. However, in one of the most blatant displays of questionable tactics ever witnessed, the rough and tough Yukon Lumberjacks took the belt away from them on June 26, 1978 in 15 minutes and 21 seconds. The Lumberjacks double-teamed DeNucci and felled him with a double axe to the throat; Pierre made the pin while the referee restrained Bravo from interfering.

Of course, since then both DeNucci and Bravo have made quite a mark in individual competition, although they still find it hard to forget the shady circumstances under which they lost that belt.

For rulebreakers, tag team competition can have great advantages, since it enables them to divide and conquer with double-team tactics. Occasionally, all four opponents wind up in the ring, and a double disqualification is announced. Such melees usually start when the rulebreaking on one side is so blatant and brutal that the fallen man's partner can no longer stand at the apron and simply watch.

Tag team competition, whether in twos, threes, or fours, is always swift and action-packed. Some teams keep their strength and stamina high with frequent tags, while others let the stronger man come in for the pin when their opponents have already been worn down. Either way, tag team fighting takes a lot of skill and studied coordination so that the team can benefit most from each man's particular strengths.

The final word on tag team competition must come from its great stars, or at least, from a small sampling of them. Some favorites in tag team events are wrestlers who actively prefer fighting with a partner. Some have had many different partners, thus showing they can work well on a team and can easily adjust to another wrestler's style. The majority, however, fare just as well in individual competition; as with any other event on a professional wrestling card, a tag team match is only as good as the grapplers participating in it.

Jack (*left*) and Jerry Brisco (*Frank Amato*)

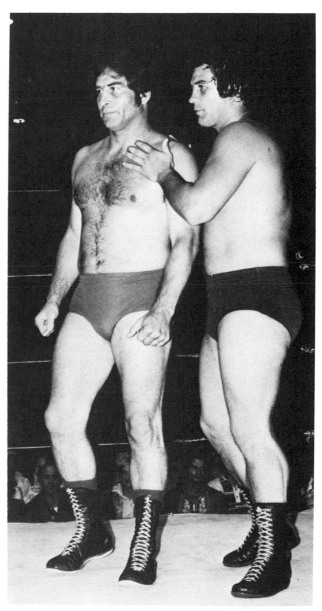

Domenic DeNucci (*George Napolitano*)

Domenic DeNucci is a veteran wrestler who is respected both in tag team and in individual competition. He has held the WWWF tag team belt first in partnership with Victor Rivera, then Pat Barrett, both back in 1975, and most recently with Dino Bravo. He says that he always fights to win a title and is just as happy to share a tag team title with a partner as he is to win a championship in his own right.

DeNucci is known to fans as a powerful (260 pounds) decent grappler who shows an incredible amount of stamina in the ring. His airplane spins, forearm smashes, armlocks, and the like have taken down many tough opponents. He is an athlete all the way, with an Olympic background to prove it.

DeNucci started his mat career in high school in Italy. In 1956 he qualified for the second string in the tryouts for the Melbourne Olympics, but didn't compete, since he couldn't raise the money for the fare to Australia.

He explains how he entered the arena of professional wrestling: "I did a lot of tournaments in England and France, after which I came to Canada, and broke into professional wrestling there."

Domenic has wrestled all over this country and the world. The constant opportunity for travel is one of the things he enjoys most about the sport. "I've been everywhere except Russia and South America," he says, "and I do believe that when you travel, you learn so many things. You meet different people and learn from them."

One thing DeNucci does not have to learn about is wrestling. Though he concentrates on his airplane spin as a finishing move, he has mastered a wide variety of other holds and maneuvers. He likes to vary his style, and considers each match a welcome challenge.

He considers Dino Bravo, Bruno Sammartino, and Ray Stevens from California to be today's top wrestlers. He also mentions his ex-partner, Victor Rivera, who now, under the tutelage of his manager Fred Blassie, has taken to breaking some rules.

"Sometimes these men are really too rough. I mean, when you wrestle a guy like that, it scares you. So many guys have been hurt . . ." He shakes his head when asked how he feels about facing the rulebreakers.

Domenic vividly recalls his major injuries—damage to the knee, arm, shoulder, several operations which almost convinced him to quit wrestling forever, and one incident in particular which he cannot forget:

"My opponent was Killer Kowalski and we were in Sydney, Australia. He really landed with a punch and my appendix burst. I almost died there."

But Domenic did come back, partly because of the fans, who he says are "the nicest people in the world" and partly because of his love for the sport. "I was ready to quit a couple of times and never go back again. Yet as soon as you feel better, you go back, because it's in your blood. But people

TAG TEAM TANDEM

often don't understand what you go through. Of course, nobody goes into that ring to kill anybody, but, believe me, it's tough.''

Domenic enjoys listening to opera, hunting, fishing, and almost all outdoor sports. ''I don't care if it's winter time, or raining, I'm always outside,'' he says. ''You see, I live on a farm in the country. I have a couple of horses, cows, dogs, chickens, and I enjoy being outdoors, working there.''

Domenic is a fine man, one could even say a gentle one. In the ring, he is also a fine sportsman, but far from gentle. Though always an honorable athlete, he is as tough as the sport which has brought him so much success.

Stan Stasiak vs. Domenic DeNucci *(Frank Amato)*

One of the men who stripped Domenic of his last WWWF tag team title is anything but gentle. Hailing from the wilds of Canada, **Eric, the Yukon Lumberjack,** along with his partner Pierre, have terrified many opponents in, and tossed many out of that squared circle. Without making unnecessary judgments, I must point out that the Lumberjacks have used any tactic they can to win.

''I don't break any rules,'' Eric insists. ''I wrestle strictly by the book.'' I must have looked at him as though one of us was crazy. Hadn't I seen him and Pierre double-team an opponent many times when the referee wasn't watching? Weren't both the experts at kicking an opponent off a fallen partner and illegally preventing a well-deserved pin?

''You can watch me in a hundred matches, and I don't pull a hair, I don't pull trunks, I don't gouge eyes . . . I don't do a lot of things. People say I break rules, but I don't. I just come out and wrestle hard,'' he insisted, with that characteristic ice in his voice. I could see we were getting nowhere. To Eric, the Lumberjacks just ''wrestle hard'' and the strategies supplied by manager Lou Albano did not constitute rulebreaking.

Eric has been in professional wrestling for over five years and has fought in arenas all over the country. In tag team competition he has met some of the best—men like Zbyszko, Calhoun, Maivia, Strongbow, Garea. But he feels that he is not being matched with opponents worthy of his abilities.

''Well, I'd like to see Bob Backlund get a decent partner and wrestle him,'' he suggests, ''or Bruno Sammartino with a good partner. I'd like to wrestle with men like Jim Brunzell, Verne Gagne, Rick Steam-

Eric of the Lumberjacks pinning Chief Jay Strongbow (*Frank Amato*)

Pierre of the Lumberjacks about to do damage to Dino Bravo (*Frank Amato*)

boat, Paul Jones . . ." One can see from this list of names that Eric is not afraid of strong competition!

In the ring Eric and Pierre have displayed a vast amount of wrestling knowledge, when not engaging in some of their more questionable moves. They are strong men (combined weight 551 pounds), big men, quick and young, and they can take a lot of punishment. Mostly though, they dish it out— with double-axes to the throat, suplexes, backbreakers, bodyslams. They tag each other frequently to keep their energy and strength levels high. "Whatever I win a match with," Eric says, "is my favorite hold for that night."

No one can deny the power of a wrestler like Eric, or of a team like the Lumberjacks. No matter how they got there, they are definitely now a legend in tag team competition, and both intend to be at the top of the wrestling world for many years to come.

TAG TEAM TANDEM

AWA contender **Greg Gagne** is definitely following in his father's footsteps. His father, of course, is the legendary Verne Gagne, one of the masters of the sport for over 30 years. And the crowds are now looking at young Greg in the same way. The 219 pound grappler from Mound, Minnesota, is known for his totally scientific orientation, his lithe frame and surprising strength, and his very high degree of stamina and courage. He is considered a top contender for the AWA championship, and has recently held the AWA tag team belt with his partner Jim Brunzell, before they were unfortunately stripped of it due to a leg injury sustained by Brunzell.

Greg loves the sport, and tells me he has been following wrestling since he was very small. "When I came out of college, I had the opportunity to play football with the Atlanta Falcons, and so I trained with my father and Billy Robinson from June of that year, both in wrestling and football. . . . When it came time to go, I decided I liked wrestling better than football."

He has been wrestling for over five years, and in that time has met many top contenders both as tag team champion and in individual competition against men like Nick Bockwinkle and Ray Stevens. He says that he could like to win either the AWA or the WWWF belt but prefers the AWA because "my father held it for such a long time." He also wants the chance to wrestle Bob Backlund again, as he did when they were both in the Minnesota area. "We had a lot of real close matches," he says.

For a young man, Greg has an impressive and effective repertoire of moves inside that ring, enjoys improvising and thrives on accepting challenges and devising new methods to defeat his foes. "I use drop

Greg Gagne (*George Napolitano*)

kicks," he tells me, "flying head scissors, and my favorite hold is the sleeper, one which I've won a lot of matches with."

Greg does not like rulebreakers, and puts them down most effectively by explaining that he feels they are merely wrestlers who lack real ability. "Basically, the wrestlers who break rules don't have a very good

Pat Patterson (*left*) vs. Jack Brisco (*Frank Amato*)

background in either amateur or professional wrestling. They're insecure in their wrestling ability."

Greg believes wrestling could be improved by national TV exposure. He suggests a program that would present great matches from all parts of the country. He tells me that 49 million people in the U.S. watch wrestling on TV—"just as many as ever turn on the Super Bowl and weekly football."

The one man Greg is after right now is Ric Flair. "We started together at the same time," he explains. "We trained together, and then he went his way, and I went mine. Now I'd definitely like to step into the ring with him." Considering the difference in

their philosophies—Greg being what he calls "an athlete" and Ric much more on the "aggressive" side—I can see a tremendously thrilling match coming up between them.

Greg has really enjoyed wrestling in tag team competition over the last three years, though he also enjoys individual matches now more and more. Basically, he loves the sport. "I've devoted my entire life to it and continually will."

When Greg and Jim Brunzell had to forfeit the AWA tag team title, the belt was awarded to the next top contenders, **Pat Patterson** and Ray Stevens. Greg says that this is one team he would like to beat, since he con-

Ray Stevens (*left*) vs. El Olympico (*George Napolitano*)

TAG TEAM TANDEM

siders them "the best team in the world for a long, long time." Patterson returns the compliment, by the way. He considers Greg and Jim Brunzell to be two of today's top wrestlers and singles out Greg as his favorite opponent.

Patterson cannot be pinned down about his style. When asked if he considers himself a rulebreaker, he ducks the question. "I'm just a wrestler," he says defensively. "I have to do everything I can to win. I don't change my style with who I wrestle. I know only one thing when I go in that ring, to give the people my best."

But some of Patterson's moves are distinctly other than scientific, like the one he calls "bombs away." "That's a kneedrop from the top rope," he explains. "Now in some rings it's not allowed, but if I have a chance to do it without the referee seeing it, I do . . . Everybody likes to break the rules. I do it and love it. But I like to get away with it, too."

Patterson says that Ray Stevens was the toughest opponent he ever faced, which is why he decided to team up with him. He tells me that Stevens is a natural wrestler. "He doesn't worry about anything. He just comes into the ring and he's one of the best in the business." He also tells me that he would probably choose Ivan Koloff or Nick Bockwinkle as alternate tag team partners. Given the philosophies of those two, one can easily see that Pat is not all that concerned with the rulebook.

Pat Patterson is a dedicated wrestler, and he hastens to explain how much effort really goes into being a professional wrestler. "People think wrestlers work 20 minutes a day. They don't know what we have to go through. Wrestlers have to travel around, making their own reservations for hotels, booking flights or buses, driving hours and hours, making sure they're at the arena on time . . . training, working, then going home to sleep and getting up and doing it all again. You don't have managers half the time, you have to work out your own contracts. When you're traveling, your wife is home all the time, and unless she has kids, she's home all alone. With football, baseball, it's a season, whereas with us it's all year round."

Whatever the difficulties, men like Pat Patterson stay in professional wrestling because they enjoy it. "I want the fans to like me," he says. "I want people to enjoy watching. Even if the crowd is not going my way, I'm going to make sure they enjoy my match."

There is one final point I'd like to make on the subject of tag teams. From what I have heard, it is obvious to me that in any event on a wrestling card there is always teamwork going on. But it is not necessarily the team that you see in the ring, but rather another one, a subtler one.

This team is made up of the wrestler who is fighting within that squared circle and the fans who sit outside it, inspiring him to go on.

Opposite: The Bruiser and the Crusher (*left*) (*George Napolitano*)

Tag Team Title Holders

World Wide Wrestling Federation Tag Team Champions

DATE	CHAMPIONS
Jun. 1971	TARZAN TYLER and LUKE GRAHAM
Dec. 1971	KARL GOTCH and RENE GOULET
Mar. 1972	KING CURTIS IAUKEA and BARON MIKEL SCICLUNA
May 1972	SONNY KING and CHIEF JAY STRONGBOW
Aug. 1972	PROFESSOR TORU TANAKA and MR. FUJI
Aug. 1973	HAYSTACKS CALHOUN and TONY GAREA
Oct. 1973	PROFESSOR TANAKA and MR. FUJI
Dec. 1973	TONY GAREA and DEAN HO
May 1974	JIMMY VALIANT and JOHNNY VALIANT
May 1975	DOMENIC DeNUCCI and VICTOR RIVERA
Jun. 1975	DOMENIC DeNUCCI and PAT BARRETT
Aug. 1975	BLACKJACK MULLIGAN and BLACKJACK LANZA
Nov. 1975	LOUIS CERDAN and TONY PARISI
Apr. 1976	THE MASKED EXECUTIONERS
Dec. 1976	CHIEF JAY STRONGBOW and BILLY WHITE WOLF
Sept. 1977	PROFESSOR TORU TANAKA and MR. FUJI
Mar. 1978	DINO BRAVO and DOMENIC DeNUCCI
Jun. 1978	THE YUKON LUMBERJACKS
Dec. 1978	TONY GAREA and LARRY ZBYSZKO

American Wrestling Association World Tag Team Titles

DATE	CHAMPIONS
Mar. 5, 1960	TINY MILLS and STAN KOWALSKI
Jul. 19, 1960	VERNE GAGNE and LEO NOMELLINI
Oct. 4, 1960	HARD BOILED HAGGERTY and LEN MONTANA
Mar. 18, 1961	HARD BOILED HAGGERTY and GENE KINISKI
May 23, 1961	WILBUR SNYDER and LEO NOMELLINI
Jul. 19, 1961	HARD BOILED HAGGERTY and GENE KINISKI
Sept. 26, 1961	HARD BOILED HAGGERTY and BOB GEIGEL
Nov. 1961	DALE LEWIS and BOBBY GRAHAM
Dec. 1961	BOB GEIGEL and OTTO VON KRUPP
Jan. 15, 1962	LARRY HENNIG and DUKE HOFFMAN

American Wrestling Association World Tag Team Titles (cont.)

DATE	CHAMPION
Feb. 13, 1962	BOB GEIGEL and STAN KOWALSKI
Apr. 1962	ART NEILSON and STAN NEILSON
Dec. 16, 1962	DOUG GILBERT and DICK STEINBORN
Jan. 1, 1963	IVAN KALMIKOFF and KAROL KALMIKOFF
Aug. 20, 1963	THE CRUSHER and DICK THE BRUISER
Feb. 9, 1964	VERNE GAGNE and MOOSE EVANS
Feb. 23, 1964	THE CRUSHER and DICK THE BRUISER
Jan. 30, 1965	LARRY HENNIG and HARLEY RACE
Jul. 24, 1965	VERNE GAGNE and THE CRUSHER
Aug. 7, 1965	HARLEY RACE and LARRY HENNIG
May 28, 1966	THE CRUSHER and DICK THE BRUISER
Jan. 6, 1967	HARLEY RACE and LARRY HENNIG
Oct. 1967	HARLEY RACE and CHRIS MARKOFF
Nov. 10, 1967	WILBUR SNYDER and PAT O'CONNOR
Dec. 2, 1967	MITSU ARAKAWA and TOR "DR. MOTO" KAMATA
Dec. 28, 1968	THE CRUSHER and DICK THE BRUISER
Aug. 30, 1969	MAD DOG VACHON and BUTCHER VACHON
May 15, 1971	RED BASTIEN and HERCULES CORTEZ
Jul. 23, 1971	RED BASTIEN and THE CRUSHER
Jan. 20, 1972	RAY STEVENS and NICK BOCKWINKLE
Jul. 21, 1974	THE CRUSHER and BILLY ROBINSON
Oct. 24, 1974	RAY STEVENS and NICK BOCKWINKLE
Aug. 16, 1975	THE CRUSHER and DICK THE BRUISER
Jul. 23, 1976	BOBBY DUNCUM and BLACKJACK LANZA
Jul. 7, 1977	JIM BRUNZELL and GREG GAGNE
Sept. 23, 1978	PAT PATTERSON and RAY STEVENS

World Tag Team Championship

DATE	CHAMPION
1957	ANTONINO ROCCA and MIGUEL PEREZ

United States Tag Team Championship

DATE	CHAMPION
1957–1958	DR. JERRY GRAHAM and EDDIE GRAHAM
1958–1959	MARK LEWIN and DON CURTIS
1959–1960	DR. JERRY GRAHAM and EDDIE GRAHAM
1960	RED BASTIEN and LOU BASTIEN
1960–1961	THE KANGAROOS
1961	BUDDY ROGERS and JOHNNIE VALENTINE
1961	THE KANGAROOS
1961–1962	JOHNNIE VALENTINE and COWBOY BOB ELLIS
1962–1963	BUDDY ROGERS and JOHNNY BAREND
1963	BUDDY AUSTIN and THE GREAT SCOTT
1963	SKULL MURPHY and BRUTE BERNARD
1963	GORILLA MONSOON and KILLER KOWALSKI
1963–1964	CHRIS TOLOS and JOHN TOLOS
1964	DON MC CLARITY and ARGENTINA APOLLO
1964	DR. JERRY GRAHAM and LUKE GRAHAM
1964	GENE KINISKI and WALDO VON ERICH
1964–1965	BILL WATTS and GORILLA MONSOON
1965–1966	DR. BILL MILLER and DAN MILLER
1966–1967	JOHNNIE VALENTINE and TONY PARISI
1967–1968	BARON MIKEL SCICLUNA and SMASHER SLOANE
1968	SPIROS ARION and TONY PARISI

International Tag Team Championship

DATE	CHAMPION
1969	PROFESSOR TORU TANAKA and MITSU ARAKAWA
1969	VICTOR RIVERA and TONY MARINO
1970	THE MONGOLS
1971	BRUNO SAMMARTINO and DOMENIC DENUCCI
1971	THE MONGOLS

4

In the Ring, On the Mat, Over for the Cover

A Sampling of Great Matches, Terrible Atrocities, and Free-for-alls

Professional wrestling is an electrifying, action-filled sport. The action is provided by the varying styles and techniques of the wrestlers themselves and the electricity starts when they step into the ring. Matches can be scientific, significant, brutal, shocking; they can display some of the finest athletic skills to be seen anywhere, or they can explode into bloody, frantic brawls.

We know that the straight match is between two opponents (or in tag team competition, four, six, or eight) each fighting for a specified length of time, with a certain number of falls deciding the winner. Simple? Never! Even these regular matches take on added color and suspense when the grapplers fighting in them are longtime rivals.

Since the beginning of time wrestlers have engaged in bitter rivalries, out of such varying motives as land (in the old days), money, honor, the battle for the belt, long-standing family feuds or simply the thirst for revenge.

The Super Destroyer once set out to annihilate Swede Hanson after a feud broke out between them. Lou Albano swore to destroy Chief Jay Strongbow. Backlund vowed revenge on Maivia. And Superstar Billy Graham has at various times called for the head of Dusty Rhodes, Harley Race, and Ken Patera. The feud between the Bruiser and the Sheik got so bad that the end of one match found them still grappling with each other, both soaked in blood, all the way back to their dressing rooms!

Sometimes special matches are held to settle these disputes or feuds, most often as the culmination of a series of hotly contested bouts between two rivals. At other times these special matches are held simply as a test of endurance or skill. These events include Texas Bull-Rope Matches, Strap Matches, Death Matches, Chain Matches,

Battle Royals, Roman Gladiator Matches, and, of course, Steel-Cage Matches.

I spoke with John Stanley, a wrestling referee for over 31 years, to find out the actual rules of some of the more popular special matches.

First we discussed the famous Steel-Cage Match, in which the ring is enclosed in a 15-foot steel cage (in the past barbed wire or chicken wire has also been used). There is no time limit and the referee's only job is to stand at the steel-bolted door of the cage in case a wrestler shouts that he wants to get out, and his opponent cannot stop him.

The object of a Steel-Cage Match is to simply get out, either through the door or over the top. Of course, a man will always try

Superstar Billy Graham raises his new belt in victory after winning the World Wide Wrestling Federation Championship from Bruno Sammartino in Baltimore on April 30, 1977. (*George Napolitano*)

to prevent his opponent from escaping, and there are virtually no rules. "They can do anything they want," Stanley tells me, "eye-gouging, punching, kicking, biting. I just hang onto the door on the outside . . . anything goes on inside."

Next the Battle Royal, which is without a doubt one of the most exciting special events to witness. Twenty men are in the ring, and the object is to get a man over the top rope. There are no teams, and the wrestlers usually try to remove the toughest men first. This process of elimination continues until only two men are left in the ring. They then wrestle to a pin. In cases where two good friends are left in the ring, they will sometimes shake hands and split the honor of winning. The winner of a Battle Royal normally has to fight the champion that same night. And you can imagine how exhausted the winner already is after eliminating 19 other wrestlers!

As with the Steel-Cage Match, the referee is on the outside and the grapplers can do anything they want; the referee only comes back into the ring for the final fall. Andre the Giant claims that he is the man the others always try to get over that top rope first. So far, no one has succeeded in tossing Andre over the top!

In the Texas Bull-Rope Match, a specialty of Texan Dusty Rhodes, each wrestler has one hand tied to one end of a bull rope which has a cowbell in the middle. A man will usually try to wrap the rope around his opponent's neck, sometimes striking him with the sharp edges of the cowbell. Again, no holds barred.

A wrestler who unties or lets go of the rope is disqualified, and a wrestler who tries to escape is simply dragged back into the ring by the man at the other end of that rope.

Opposite: Ernie Ladd vs. Ray Candy in a Steel-Cage Match (*George Napolitano*)

Over the top rope—Tony Garea at the mercy of Spiros Arion in a Battle Royal (*Frank Amato*)

Needless to say, these matches often end in bloody messes!

The Indian Death Match uses a strap instead of a rope and is equally free from rules. Chief Jay Strongbow, appropriately enough, is one of the specialists in this field.

A Chain Match is fought on the same principle, except that sometimes the chain that links the two contestants is used to choke the opponent and hold him down for a pin—or whatever punishment the victor has prepared for his rival.

These special matches are filled with emotion and with action. They usually end with a lot of blood, and either a lot of cheers or a lot of controversy.

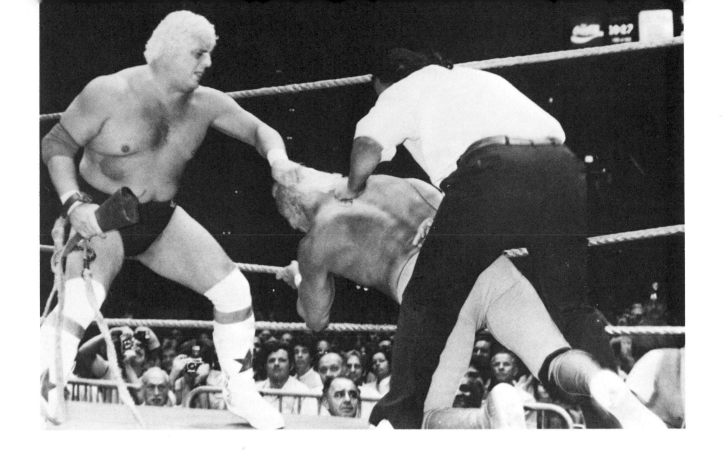

Dusty Rhodes holds the cowbell over Billy Graham in a Texas Bull-Rope Match. Chief Jay Strongbow referees. (*Frank Amato*)

Wahoo McDaniel over Billy Graham in a Strap Match (*George Napolitano*)

Jose Lothario vs. Bull Ramos in a Chain Match (*George Napolitano*)

One particularly interesting special match took place between Pedro Morales, before he won the WWWF championship, and the infamous Sheik, former United States Heavyweight Champion, on September 5, 1969. This was a "Sicilian Stretcher Death Match," with the following rules:

*No disqualification
*No count-out
*No pin falls
*No holds barred
*Doctor cannot stop bout
*No referee in ring
*No surrender
*Loser carried out

Anyone can see that they meant business in this encounter!

The battle quickly flared as the Sheik and his manager, Abdullah Farouk, started to attack Morales as he turned to remove his jacket. Pedro flew into action, throwing Farouk from the ring, cornering the Sheik, ripping off his headdress, and pummeling his body.

The Sheik crawled out under the ropes and onto the apron, with Morales in hot pursuit. Pedro decided to treat the Sheik to some of his own medicine by resorting to eye-gouging. But Morales was distracted by Farouk, and the dazed Sheik managed to crawl back to the center of the ring. The referee rolled him onto a stretcher while the crowd cheered.

Suddenly, the Sheik jumped off the mat and looked around for Farouk, who handed his man a sharp pencil to use for "protection." Morales charged across the ring, only to be met with a piercing jab to the throat from the concealed weapon! Morales dropped to the mat and rolled over in agony. With his eyes glazed over like a madman's, the Sheik rammed the pencil repeatedly into Pedro's exposed neck.

Fighting for his life, Pedro Morales threw a deadly punch at the Sheik. The pencil rolled out of his hand and Pedro picked it up, gouging the eyes, mouth, and neck of the Lebanese trickster.

At this point, Farouk grabbed Morales by the legs and pulled him out of the ring; still clutching the pencil, Morales grabbed Farouk, ready to deliver a well-deserved punch.

But the blow never came, for the Sheik had gotten to his feet, grabbed a steel chair, and sent it crashing off the back of Morales's head.

Morales hit the floor with a thud and crumpled into a heap. He was carried out, still unconscious. The Sheik and Abdullah

The Sheik gouges the eyes of Pedro Morales. (*George Napolitano*)

Farouk scurried back to their dressing rooms triumphantly.

Pedro Morales was to prove his great skill later, on the night of September 30, 1972, when he met Bruno Sammartino for one of the greatest scientific matches in wrestling history.

Morales, who was then WWWF Champion, and Bruno, who had been champion for so many years (and who was later to win that belt back from Stan Stasiak, the man who defeated Morales), wrestled to over a one hour draw. When the match ended, Sammartino embraced Morales and raised the champion's hand. The crowd that filled Shea Stadium that night knew that it was seeing an extraordinary combination of skill and professionalism.

Most matches that involved Bruno Sammartino were exciting, alive with the super-strength and skill of the Living Legend of professional wrestling. But one in particular has special significance—the match in which Bruno had his revenge on Stan Hansen!

It was in April 1976 that Sammartino first defended his belt against the brutal Texan. Throughout most of the battle Bruno had the upper hand. Then Hansen bodyslammed Bruno and the champion landed in an unfortunate way, his head and one shoulder hitting the mat sideways. Bruno felt the pain and thought he heard a crack, but he was determined to keep on wrestling.

He battled on, and suddenly the match turned in Hansen's favor. Then came the fatal moment when Hansen applied his famous lariat, in which the Texan armwhips his opponent off the ropes and swings a padded elbow into his neck or head.

Several seconds later, the doctor told the referee to stop the match. Bruno was bleed-

ing badly, and he nearly collapsed in his dressing room. He was taken to the hospital, where X-rays showed that he had sustained several broken vertebrae in his neck and back—in other words, his neck was broken.

He was put into traction for four weeks and spent more time just lying on his back in the hospital or at home.

When he was finally able to rise, Sammartino went into intensive training again. Two weeks later, he issued a challenge to Hansen for a rematch. Bruno told the press that he was burning for revenge.

The match took place at Shea Stadium on June 25, 1976, as a special event before the closed-circuit broadcast of the Muhammad Ali-Antonio Inoki bout from Japan. Bruno tore into Hansen from the outset; he seemed to turn savage in this bout, which many fans felt was entirely understandable. Time after time Hansen was knocked from the ring, and many times he fled from the ring to escape further punishment. Hansen tried to apply his lariat twice and failed. Bruno had learned how to counter it.

Now Bruno tore the elbow pad from Hansen's left arm. Using it like a boxing glove, he ripped into Hansen with blow after blow. Blood covered Stan's face; he fell to the mat and finally Hansen ran from the ring.

The feud was brought to its conclusion in a Steel-Cage match in Madison Square Garden on August 7 of the same year. It was only the second such match in Garden history; in the first, just eight months earlier, Bruno had defeated Ivan Koloff. In this bout Bruno also triumphed; he left Hansen lying on the mat as he walked proudly out of the cage door.

A few years and two champions later, still another feud was settled in that same cage. On the night of April 24, 1978, again in Mad-

Stan Hansen is all over Thunderbolt Patterson. (*George Napolitano*)

Bruno Sammartino locks on to Bobby Duncum. (*George Napolitano*)

ison Square Garden, Bob Backlund met Superstar Billy Graham within that steel encasing to settle the dispute over who was champion. Backlund had won the WWWF belt from Graham in February, but at the time of the pin it seemed as though Graham's leg was over the rope. Another match was held to settle the dispute, and because that was stopped, it was inconclusive. So a Steel-Cage Match was called for.

Graham was a veteran of these matches. Backlund was not. The fans were on the edge of their seats, hopeful, yet also fearing the worst.

When Backlund stepped into the cage, Graham charged him and drove a knee into his head. The battle had begun. Superstar came at Bob with knees and fists and he staggered under the attack. Then Graham armwhipped his opponent headfirst into the

IN THE RING, ON THE MAT, OVER FOR THE COVER

steel mesh. Graham tried to climb out of the cage but Bob grabbed his tights and pulled him down. Now Backlund launched his own attack, playing as rough as Graham ever could. Kicks and punches were the predominant maneuvers.

Each wrestler took turns battering the other, but neither one had a clear edge. Each man tried twice to make it over the top; three times one or the other tried to get through the door. And as the battering continued both wrestlers began to show its effects. Both men were breathing heavily, obviously exhausted.

Backlund caught Graham from behind and used his atomic knee-drop. It looked like the end for Graham as Bob made for the door, but Graham, crawling on his hands and knees, caught him and viciously pulled him back.

The fans knew by now that they were watching a classic match between two strong and determined men. Backlund bounced Graham off the steel mesh and the Superstar came up bloody. He was hurt. Bob pressed this attack and drove Graham again and again into the mesh; blood was now streaming from his face.

Still Graham did not give up; he fought back furiously. A flurry of blows and a powerful bodyslam left Backlund reeling. Graham tried for the door again but was yanked back.

Then, Backlund drove Graham headfirst into the steel. Graham landed almost upside down, and as he tried to right himself his left

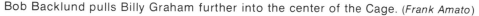

Bob Backlund pulls Billy Graham further into the center of the Cage. (*Frank Amato*)

leg became lodged between the ring and the cage. It was obvious that the Superstar was now at the young champion's mercy.

After hesitating several seconds, Backlund left the Superstar where he was, deciding not to inflict any more punishment on him, and walked out the door—the undisputed champion at last. The match was far more grueling and exciting than the crowd had expected, as Backlund proved his stamina inside that steel cage.

Though beaten conclusively in a Steel-Cage Match, Billy Graham certainly didn't contemplate giving up his fighting career. He also proved his toughness and strength that night. And he was as ready as ever to take on any challenger.

One of Billy's frequent opponents and also rivals is the American Dream, Dusty Rhodes. One of Dusty Rhodes's closest friends is Andre the Giant, and everyone knew that a match which featured Billy fighting Dusty with Andre as referee would be anything but dull.

Dusty and Billy had already met on several occasions in Texas Bull-Rope matches, and though most ended inconclusively with both wrestlers soaked with blood, Dusty always seemed to have had the upper hand in these affairs.

Because of the savagery of their encounters, Andre seemed like a good choice to keep order in the ring. He knew that he could grant no special favors to Dusty and that he would have to be as fair as he could to Billy Graham.

Dusty didn't look at Andre when he walked into the ring. Neither did Graham. At the start of the match Billy came out and kicked Dusty in the thigh, a clear violation of the rules. When Andre tried to intervene, Billy denounced him loudly for showing fa-

Billy Graham (*left*) and Dusty Rhodes in a cowbell encounter with Chief Jay Strongbow as referee (*Frank Amato*)

voritism and went on a rampage. Dusty rarely got a chance to fight off the kicks and blows. Finally, when he could stand it no longer, Dusty went completely berserk and Andre had no choice but to disqualify him.

The whole encounter, as is usual between these two, was a flurry of action, an unrelenting battle of attack and counterattack. These are two grapplers who fight every second they can, and the excitement rarely lets up.

IN THE RING, ON THE MAT, OVER FOR THE COVER

As far as excitement is concerned, few wrestlers can top Mil Mascaras. His holds and maneuvers are so quick, so varied, that his opponents are often dazed and confused, and become desperately frustrated by his catlike ability to slip out of any hold.

Mascaras met a true challenge in Boston in 1978, when he encountered the heart punch specialist, former WWWF champion Stan "the Man" Stasiak.

At the opening bell, Mil bolted out of his corner and surprised Stasiak with one of his famous flying dropkicks. Stan fled from the ring to recuperate, then leapt back in to surprise Mascaras with a foot to the midsection. Mil bent over in pain and Stasiak pummeled his back with his fists. Suddenly

Mil Mascaras headlocks Stan Stasiak. (*Frank Amato*)

Mascaras reached down, tripped Stasiak, and snapped on a painful arm bar.

For the next five minutes the masked man dominated the bout with a series of arm and leglocks, until Stasiak forced a break by grabbing the ropes. Mil leapt quickly to his feet and delivered a flying head-scissors.

Mil Mascaras, with as many holds as he has masks, moved around the ring like lightning. He threw Stasiak into the ropes, but Stan bounced back and clamped on a bearhug. After three minutes Stasiak decided his opponent was nearly finished. He released his hold so he could deliver that devastating heart punch, which turned out to be a mistake.

One blow landed, but Mil was still on his feet. As Stan was getting ready to deliver a second punch Mil flipped him, ran into the ropes, and delivered a perfectly executed dropkick.

Stasiak fell to the mat. Mil lifted him up, threw him into the ropes, and caught him right across the chin with a body tackle. Then, for the famous Mascaras finishing move, Mil climbed onto the ropes and dove right into the stunned Stasiak. Stan fell to the mat, the referee counted to three. The masked man was victorious once again, and Stasiak was given a lesson in wrestling he would not soon forget—any more than Ernie Ladd, the ex-football player from Houston, will forget his 1972 match with Dory Funk, Jr., the then-current NWA heavyweight champion.

At the sound of the bell, Dory charged across the ring and threw Ladd to the canvas. He applied an armlock, but it didn't last for long; Ladd gouged Dory's eyes, and Funk was forced to release the hold. While Funk was trying to recover against the ropes, Ladd threw several body blocks to

Ernie Ladd views the helpless Dusty Rhodes. (*Frank Amato*)

the midsection, then tormented Funk with rabbit-punches, headlocks, and illegal choke holds. Ladd felt he was only seconds away from the championship, but Dory was not about to lose his grip on the title.

Summoning up his remaining strength, Funk sent a powerful punch to Ladd's face and knocked him to the mat. Ladd got up while the exhausted Funk was still sagging against the ropes, charged across and caught Dory in a powerful bearhug. Funk cunningly responded by clapping his arms together against Ladd's ears.

Funk followed through with a kneelift that caught Ladd flush in the face while he was still doubled over in pain. The Big Cat went down.

For the next several minutes neither man could gain an advantage. Ladd tried his deadly karate thumb thrust, along with more choke holds, and soon it looked like the Big Cat had the match sewed up. Again and again, Funk tried to rise and take over, only to be brutally thrown back down to the mat by the gigantic Ladd.

Suddenly, the wounded Funk rose from the mat, lifted 315-pound Ernie Ladd into the air for a knee drop. Furious, Funk crashed his knee into the small of Ladd's back. He then lifted the big man up by the hair and drove a fist into his nose. Ladd reeled back and countered with a kick to his opponent's head, which drove Dory through the ropes and out onto the apron. Ladd then reached

IN THE RING, ON THE MAT, OVER FOR THE COVER

over, grabbed Dory in a headlock, and flipped him over the ropes back into the ring.

As Funk struggled helplessly, Ladd applied a backbreaker hold. Hoisting him over his shoulder like a rag doll, Ladd increased the pressure and it looked like the champion was about to concede.

In one last valiant effort, Funk thrashed around furiously, which knocked Ladd off balance. He wobbled unsteadily over to the corner turnbuckle; Funk managed to get a toehold on the top buckle and gave a great heave that sent them both crashing to the mat. The impact left Ladd breathless and Funk wound up on the top, easily making the pin.

As you can see, when one excellent grappler meets another, the contest is challenging, brutal, and exhausting. But what about when it's 19 against 1?

A 1977 Battle Royal held in Boston brought these men into one ring: Ken Pa-tera, the Executioners, Nikolai Volkoff, Stan Stasiak, Bruiser Frank Brody, Tor Kamata, Billy White Wolf, Chief Jay Strongbow, Larry Zbyszko, Doug Gilbert, S.D. Jones, Pete Sanchez, Pat Patterson, Johnny Rodz, Jose Gonzales, Baron Scicluna, Manuel Soto, Tony Altimore, and Johnny Rivera.

They entered the ring one by one, all looking tense but determined. The ring announcer read the rules for the benefit of the crowd:

(1) The only way a man can be eliminated is to be tossed out of the ring over the top ropes.
(2) No holds barred. Anything goes inside the ring.
(3) Three referees will supervise the match, all officiating from outside the ring.
(4) When only two men remain, there will be a rest period, followed by a one-fall-to-a-finish bout to find a winner.

Dory Funk, Jr., has control. (*George Napolitano*)

Baron Mikel Scicluna and big Crusher Blackwell double-team Dino Bravo. (*Frank Amato*)

Luke Graham, Spiros Arion, and Crusher Blackwell all pitch in to get Gorilla Monsoon
over that top rope. (*Frank Amato*)

Then the announcer called for the bell and the match was on!

The sight in the ring was unbelievable. Fans did not know where to look. Larry Zbyszko went after Ken Patera. Chief Jay Strongbow and Billy White Wolf battled with their arch enemies, the Executioners. Johnny Rodz was after Tony Altimore, and Altimore was the first victim to be tossed out of the ring, followed quickly by Johnny Rivera, who was thrown out by Doug Gilbert.

Then, in the middle of the ring, the Executioners left Strongbow and White Wolf and started double-teaming their own stable-mate, Ken Patera! Patera was shocked, but he recovered quickly enough to start throwing punches and kicks at the masked men. The others stopped to watch the three Albano protégés slug it out. Nikolai Volkoff and Stan Stasiak broke up the unexpected battle.

Then, the Executioners charged Bruiser Frank Brody. They lifted him up and tossed him over the top ropes. S. D. Jones and Manuel Soto were the next to be eliminated, thanks to Nikolai Volkoff. Just as Ken Patera was speeding Pat Patterson over the ropes, Larry Zbyszko and José Gonzales crept up

IN THE RING, ON THE MAT, OVER FOR THE COVER

behind him, and a double dropkick sent one of the world's strongest men flying out of the ring.

The Executioners and the Indians were still involved in their slugfest when Pete Sanchez and Larry Zbyszko caught them by surprise and shoved all four over the top ropes. Sanchez then went for his rival, Johnny Rodz, and dropkicked him out of the battle; Larry Zbyszko did the same to Baron Scicluna, leaving only six men in the ring.

Zbyszko turned around, though, and walked right into a vicious judo chop from Tor Kamata which sent him flying from the ring. Sanchez was tossed out by Nikolai Volkoff. This left Stan Stasiak, Nikolai Volkoff, and Tor Kamata against young José Gonzales. José was backed into a corner by the three huge grapplers. Then, Jose shot out of the corner and launched a barrage of dropkicks. One hit Kamata in the jaw, eliminating him. José aimed another dropkick at Stan Stasiak, missed, and landed sprawling on the mat. Volkoff and Stasiak took advantage of this and began to kick José until he almost lost consciousness, then picked him up and threw him over the ropes.

Stasiak and Volkoff were left alone in the ring. Sure, they were close friends, but the winner of the Battle Royal would get a crack at WWWF champion Bruno Sammartino later that night. Could either one turn down such an opportunity for friendship's sake?

The two men started circling each other, looking back and forth from the crowds to the challenge awaiting them in the ring. Then Stan offered his hand in friendship and Volkoff cautiously accepted it. They asked the referee to flip a coin. Volkoff won the toss, and later that night went against Bruno Sammartino for the championship. You could tell the Mongolian Giant was worn out

from his Battle Royal. Bruno defeated him in only 10 minutes.

Of course, literally hundreds of thrilling and significant matches have occurred in wrestling history. Most people have one or two they particularly remember, either because of the excitement or the winner or the unusual circumstances that surrounded the match. It would be impossible even to come close to naming the "greatest matches"—there have been so many.

One thing can be said, though—very few professional wrestling matches are dull. When good grapplers enter that ring they fight long and hard, and display all the knowledge of the sport they have ac-

Pat Patterson about to ram the head of Jack Brisco into solid steel (*Frank Amato*)

Bob Backlund pins Superstar Billy Graham for the World Wide Wrestling Federation Championship in New York City on February 20, 1978. (*Frank Amato*)

cumulated over the years. And in cases of bitter rivalries they sometimes add the tinder of emotion to fire that determined skill!

There are special matches, tag matches, challenge matches, bitter ones, and scientifically excellent ones. They are all exciting. And the most exciting moment in any match comes when one opponent covers another, pins his shoulders to the canvas, and the referee slams that mat for a full count of three!

5

The Men Who Make Wrestlers

There is no getting away from the fact that the stars of wrestling are the fiber, the blood, and the action of every match. But there are many others who rarely appear in the ring, or do so only in a secondary role, who have as much to do with the sport as the wrestlers themselves.

First, there are the promoters and administrators. These men are often blamed for a variety of sins, the most critical being that they don't match up the right opponents. But the final word I have to offer on that score is something a wrestling enthusiast once said to me, and I believe it's true—"The promoters don't make the matches, the fans do." The promoters' great achievement is bringing wrestling into top arenas all across the country, so that millions of fans can easily see and enjoy their favorite stars in action.

Next, there are the referees, men like John Stanley, Dick Wirley, Dick Crow, Red Shoes Dugan; the list is so long that it is almost shameful to mention one without listing them all. These men are also criticized by rulebreakers, scientific wrestlers, managers, and fans for their judgment in that ring. But theirs is an extremely hard job, and they do their very best. No matter how quick or eagle-eyed the referee might be, he can-

not be two places at once and he cannot see everything. He does what he thinks is fair and most often he is right. And contrary to some people's complaints, I have never seen a referee favoring one wrestler over another

The referee tries to prevent Ox Baker from choking the life out of Jimmy Snuka. (*George Napolitano*)

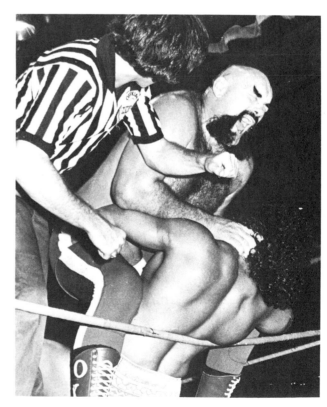

for any other reason than their conduct— that is, the referee judges a match according to the rules and to the way wrestlers in the ring conform to them.

The third group that perform their magic behind the scenes are the all-important managers. These are the men who find the talent and cultivate it. They train their wrestlers, advise them, sometimes take them down to the gym and train alongside them. They, too, have different methods, styles, techniques and philosophies, and they certainly add on many occasions, both by their seen and unseen presence, a lot of the color and excitement that is professional wrestling.

These men, like Arnold Skaaland, Lou Albano, Bobby Heenan, the Grand Wizard, and Fred Blassie, have to know an incredible amount about their sport to be able to train and advise the men they manage. They have many good points to make about wrestling, and in this chapter I have chosen to let them make these points for themselves. In talking to them I have found that they are more responsible for the successes of their protégés than one might think.

It takes a lot of time, effort, and energy to make up a great wrestling card. Of course, the fourth group that works behind the scenes is probably the most important. It's the fans.

Captain Lou Albano

Sitting with the man electric—that's how it feels. There is a vibration in the air, one of excitement, of force, of charged power. Some people call him a lunatic, others say he is vicious, uncouth; the fans jeer at him, guards carry him kicking and struggling out of the ring, some wrestlers call him a disgrace to the sport. But his skill and knowledge have helped create seven world tag team champions. And if nothing else, Lou Albano is the Captain.

"I am a man to be reckoned with," he says excitedly, for he does and says few things calmly. "I have proved myself time and time again, 25 years in the wrestling business and 11 years as a professional manager; I feel I know all the pitfalls and weaknesses in opponents and I look for them . . . then I point these flaws out to my men and therefore I'm able to give them a little something extra."

A *little* something extra? No, Lou Albano does nothing if it isn't all the way. He handles top men in the sport, champions like Ivan Koloff, the Lumberjacks, the Valiant Brothers, George Steele, and a host of others. He bends rules, breaks rules, and when it suits him, makes new ones.

"Well, as far as rulebreaking goes, I'll tell you the truth. I'm looking to make money, more or less, and I don't care about rules. I believe there's only one way and it's the winning way."

Even when Lou is relatively calm, he is still on fire. His unkempt appearance, his long, loose hair, the way his voice always seems to be on the verge of going out of control, cause many to label him "the wild man of wrestling." Well, wild or not, he seems to coach for success.

"I've had Ivan Koloff beat Bruno Sammartino for the WWWF championship, I've had the Lumberjacks, tag team champions, and the Valiants. Seven tag team champions in all. I specialized in the tag team. But right now, in the near future, I have a surprise in store for the WWWF and I can't say who it's with, but this man will be *my* champion."

Albano praises his stable of wrestlers endlessly. He cites their strength, stamina, and particularly their aggressiveness. He trains them that way, and he trains them hard. He explains that Koloff never won the title back simply because he got "cocky" and failed to listen to him. "He didn't follow my rules. He was perhaps a little overconfident and didn't listen to the Captain."

How anyone couldn't listen to the Captain when he speaks is beyond me. Sometimes he sounds like a possessed man. "I am the Captain, I am the guiding light, I am the maker of world champions, and I've got a lot more surprises in store! Watch out for the Captain, because I am a scientific genius. I said I'm a mental strategist, I fill in matches entirely." When he tells me how he secretly tapes the matches fought by his wrestlers' prospective opponents, and how he does it by sneaking in dressed as an old lady, I wonder about somebody's sanity. A bearded man who weighs over 250 pounds doesn't really pull that kind of thing off!

But it is amazing how much Albano can pull off, especially with the rigorous routines he imposes on his wrestlers. "You must have strength, size, ability, fortitude, wrestling knowledge, wrestling balance, and wrestling ability to be a world champion," he explains, and then proceeds to tell me

Managers in question (*standing from left to right*)—the Grand Wizard of Wrestling and Fred Blassie, (*kneeling*) Captain Lou Albano (*Frank Amato*)

THE MEN WHO MAKE WRESTLERS

how he tries to encourage these qualities in his army!

"I like my men to stay on a strict carbohydrate-free diet, much, much protein, stay away from alcoholic beverages. I don't like to see them smoke. I like them to do 7 to 10 miles a day of roadwork, do a lot of weight training. I like them to perform repetition of curls; I like them to bench press 250 to 300 pounds. I like them to get out and train 3 or 4 times a week. I'll take Ivan and put him against Pierre of the Lumberjacks and have them get out and sit out on each other and perform a suplex and get down and chicken wing . . . and perform a head scissors . . . I'll point out their weakness and . . ."

Albano goes on like this, and one can easily see how fanatically dedicated he is to what he does. He is also dedicated to provoking other people. Billy White Wolf, Chief Jay Strongbow, Bob Backlund, and Arnold Skaaland (who finally fought him and won in a grudge match), can all attest to the way Albano can taunt a man.

I remember that when Backlund won a press photographers' award, Albano and his protégé George Steele set upon Bob, smashing the trophy, ripping the clothes from his back, and beating on him mercilessly. Yet when speaking about Backlund, Albano sings a different tune.

"I believe this young Backlund is a very good scientific wrestler with speed, agility, power, the man has it all together. He weighs 239 and stands 6 foot 2 and I feel perhaps he's a coming Bruno Sammartino . . . he doesn't have many weaknesses . . . he's a tough man to beat." I must have looked startled, but the Captain went on to confuse me further with his praise of Sammartino, another man he once seemed bent on destroying.

"Sammartino is in his own right a great wrestler, he's in such fine condition. I would have to say there are many great wrestlers, but I'd have to put Sammartino in as one of the greatest."

Albano even admits that George Steele, one of his own boys, and cited by many grapplers as the most vicious in that ring, is a little uncontrollable. After all, he is known as "the Animal." "George Steele is a very unique type of personality; he's tough to control. He's a very emotional type person. At times he has schizophrenic, homicidal tendencies, but, whatever, he's a big strong man."

Albano obviously does recognize wrestling ability. As he's already told me, he's been in the sport for 25 years. He tells me about 1946 and '47 with Gorgeous George, Antonino Rocca, Gene Stanley, Tarzan Hewitt; the old days with Frank Judson, Stanislaus Zbyszko, Jim Londos, Strangler Ed Lewis, Joe Stecker.

"Then coming up to the modern era," he continues. "From Buddy Rogers into Bruno Sammartino, a living legend, 14 years a world's champion, then Koloff, who took the belt away from Bruno, back into Pedro Morales, who was a great champion, back into Stasiak, who beat Morales, back into right up to the present when you come into Bob Backlund; or any man that can win the world championship has got to be a well-qualified, well-groomed, well-conditioned athlete . . ."

The Captain is obviously possessed by the sport. I feel like offering him a chapter to write himself as he goes on with his capsule histories. But there is no getting away from it—he knows more than just names and figures. He knows how to wrestle, because, rulebreakers or not, his champions know

Albano's "protégé," Ivan Koloff, devastating yet another opponent. (*George Napolitano*)

how to win. He, of course, claims that it all comes from him.

Though wrestling fans don't care that much for Albano, he doesn't seem to realize it. "I'm proud to have them behind me," he says smugly. By this time I'm tired of being so confused. "I know they all love the Captain. The fans out there, they realize greatness. They appreciate the great talent of Lou Albano . . ."

He's starting again, I can tell, so I just listen to see what's coming next. "They know within my own right I am immortal. I am a genius. I've got it all together." It wouldn't make much difference if I disagreed with him. He probably wouldn't hear me. So I just nod.

This prompts him to lean forward and pronounce, "You see, I'm one of a kind. I'm often imitated but never duplicated." On that score I do wholeheartedly agree with the Captain.

Fred Blassie

"Classy" Freddie Blassie, the Hollywood Fashion Plate, is not one of the most popular people with the fans of professional wrestling. In fact, one could say that he is one of the most unpopular—both with the fans and with the group of scientific grapplers who are known for their sportsmanship. He not only manages rulebreakers, but he also takes pride in turning scientific wrestlers into rulebreakers with promises of gold and glory. He taunts his boys' opponents both in and out of the arena, and sometimes uses his famous cane to do further damage to a man when one of his wrestlers has thrown him out of the ring and into Blassie's corner.

Yet when Muhammad Ali agreed to wrestle Antonio Inoki in Japan, he chose Fred Blassie as his guide and trainer. Why? Because along with the Blassie belligerence and ruthlessness goes the skill. Fred Blassie has only been a top wrestling manager for four years or so. Before that he was one of the top wrestlers in the world.

Blassie has held five world heavyweight titles; he's faced every top wrestling name you could think of in the last quarter century. His name alone on a wrestling card always insured a sellout. As a wrestler, he was a villain's villain, respected and feared by friend and foe alike. His tours of Japan were some of the wildest and roughest on record.

In the Orient he was known as a "vampire," because he used his teeth in a match as much as his arms and legs. His no-holds-barred style has now been transferred to the top grapplers he manages—men like Spiros Arion, Victor Rivera, and his most recent addition, High Chief Peter Maivia.

The first man he brought into the ring was Nikolai Volkoff. With him Blassie established his managing style, which wasn't much different from his wrestling style. When a choice had to be made between scientific holds or rough, aggressive tactics, Blassie always advised his men to use the latter.

After bringing Volkoff from Siberia to the WWWF in early 1974, Blassie led a succession of awesome men into that squared circle—like Shozo "Strong" Kobayashi in 1974, The Wolfman in 1975, and Waldo Von Erich from Germany.

Blassie is still obsessed with the WWWF belt, which has eluded him as wrestler and manager for over 14 years. "As a pro wrestler, I never did win that title of recognition . . . just a smaller version in 1959 when I beat Edouard Carpentier. In 1974, I failed to beat Sammartino, in '72 and '73 failed against Morales . . . but I didn't lose those matches. The belt was kept from me on technicalities."

So Blassie spends every minute trying to make sure his stable of wrestlers are ready to take that belt away when the time is right. Though he likes being a wrestler "a thousand times more than being a manager," it would be worth it all if he could guide a man to that belt.

Blassie does not wrestle anymore because of severe injuries, primarily to his legs. "I've had three knee operations and needed a fourth. A good friend of mine makes a revolutionary mold that goes inside the shoe so that now I don't have to limp around," he explains.

Fred Blassie poses menacingly with Victor Rivera. (*George Napolitano*)

THE MEN WHO MAKE WRESTLERS

Blassie is so determined that he has even contemplated getting back into the ring himself, injured or not. "I see a bunch of these dingalings out there calling themselves wrestlers . . . I can snuff them up one nostril and blow them out the other."

Blassie is also an outspoken champion of ruthlessness in the ring: "I tell my boys to go out there and win. I don't care what tactics they use, if they had to hit their mother in the nose or their grandmother or whoever . . . it makes no difference, just so they win. You make money by winning and I love to win: I've always hated a loser. Anybody can be a loser."

Fred does everything to insure that his boys do not lose, even illegally helping them out when he can by striking fallen opponents. During a match between Spiros Arion and Chief Jay Strongbow, he attacked the chief and ripped his headdress to shreds. He has done as much, or more, to other decent grapplers.

I ask Fred if anyone had ever called him out on his outrageous behavior. "Wrestlers have second thoughts before attacking me," he replies haughtily. "They know I'll resort to anything—bites, kicks, eye gouges . . . I'll stick my cane down their throats. As you can see"—he flashes a ten-carat diamond ring—"I'm even well fortified in jewelry."

Blassie doesn't really like anyone, other than his boys. He says referees are "useless, like a fifth post in the ring," that scientific wrestlers are "namby-pamby boys who figure they have to abide by the rules to win," and that fans are "pencil-necked geeks."

Fred Blassie is certainly not known for his modesty. He informs me that he has just cut a pop music record out on the West Coast—more proof of how he can do anything a thousand times better than anyone else. His answer was predictable when I asked him how he thought wrestling could be improved. "Only one way," he said. "Have another Freddie Blassie in that ring, but that's an impossibility. There's only one Blassie in a lifetime and nobody, nobody has ever been more vicious in the ring than myself!"

Another of Blassie's Army, Spiros Arion, attacks Dusty Rhodes. (*Frank Amato*)

Bobby Heenan

The last few years have been good to Bobby "the Brain" Heenan. On November 8, 1975, in St. Paul, Minnesota, Heenan became manager of the AWA Heavyweight Champion when Nick Bockwinkle defeated Verne Gagne. Heenan then went on to become manager of the tag team champions on July 23, 1976, when Blackjack Lanza and Bobby Duncum upset the team of the Crusher and the Bruiser.

Many people say Heenan doesn't deserve this kind of luck.

He is known for instructing his wrestlers in somewhat dubious tactics, for smuggling questionable "objects" into the ring, and for interfering in matches when things are not going his way.

Whether this is true or not, he was named manager of the year in 1977, if only in recognition of the impressive list of grapplers he has handled—among them Lanza, Blackjack Mulligan, Handsome Jimmy Valiant, Luscious John Valiant, Ivan Koloff, Ernie Ladd, Baron von Raschke, and Lord Alfred Hayes.

Heenan's group, which he refers to as his "stable of champions," has gone through many changes over the years, but the caliber of his wrestlers has always remained high. Whatever the level of their tactics and sportsmanship, they are certainly at the top of the sport.

Heenan, who once wrestled himself under the name "Pretty Boy," now devotes most of his time and energies to managing. Now he is content just to sit back and only gets into the ring when one of his wrestlers is in trouble, which usually turns the tide in favor of his man.

It should be noted that Bobby Heenan has shed more blood than any other professional wrestling manager in the history of the sport. This is often because he provokes his wrestlers' opponents to use the same interfering and aggressive tactics on him that he illegally tries to use on them.

His history of managing champions, however, is almost unbeatable. Before Lanza and Duncum, there was the AWA championship tag team of Nick Bockwinkle and Ray Stevens, whom he started to manage in 1974. Before that he had the team of Blackjack Lanza and Blackjack Mulligan, who have held several tag team titles.

In addition, Bobby has guided the careers of Chris Markoff and Angelo Poffo, the team known as "the Devil's Duo." Baron von Raschke won a major title in Detroit while under the guidance of "the Brain."

Many people also feel that Heenan is the real power behind Nick Bockwinkle. Bockwinkle constantly seeks out his advice, and those in the know say that he will never attempt a move without Heenan's approval. Bobby's tricky and carefully planned-out strategy has been called the key to his lineup of title winners.

Ray Stevens, once known as "the Crippler," is one wrestler who has had a falling out with the whole Heenan family, and though his tactics are still sometimes held in question, his philosophy of winning has softened considerably since leaving the clan.

Bobby Heenan is definitely a driving manager, an awesome power, who lets his opinions and voice be heard. In fact, nearly 75 percent of his injuries have occurred while

Bobby "the Brain" Heenan (*Frank Amato*)

he has been shouting instructions to his wrestlers from ringside, or when he hops into the ring to help them out.

People have labeled him the most hated manager in the AWA. Remember, he has also been named manager of the year. There is one thing that cannot be questioned. When his wrestlers are in the ring, Bobby Heenan is in there 100 percent in spirit (and about 75 percent in person).

One of Heenan's stable of champions was Blackjack Mulligan, shown here with the edge on Bruno Sammartino. (*George Napolitano*)

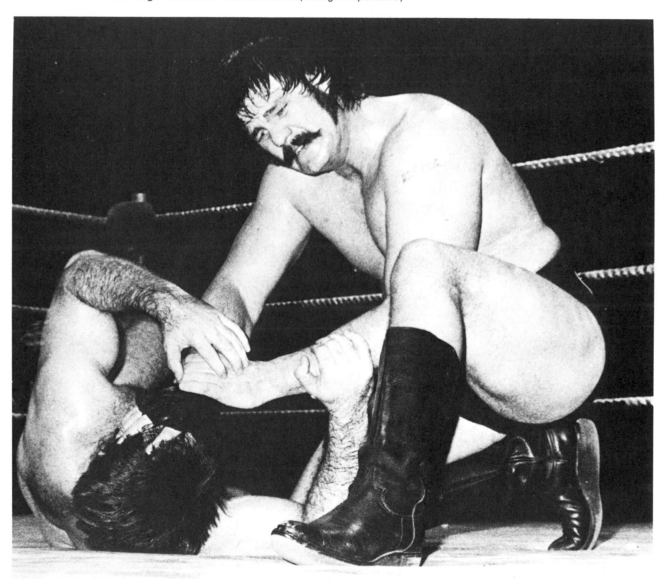

Arnold Skaaland

If any man knows the world of professional wrestling, it's Arnold Skaaland. A wrestler for close to 35 years, a man who has grappled with the greats—Lou Thesz, Buddy Rogers, Jim Londos—a fine athlete and a gentleman who is respected throughout the sport, Arnold is best known today as the man who manages champions. He is responsible for much of the power and knowledge behind the Living Legend, Bruno Sammartino, and the talented WWWF belt holder, Bob Backlund.

Though Skaaland, known as the "Golden Boy" of wrestling throughout his career, seldom dons the tights these days, he was once considered to be no less than the very best. He holds many records which are yet to be broken; for example, he is the only wrestler who was never defeated in Madison Square Garden (having fought in about 100 bouts in that arena). He was Pacific Coast Champion, and has wrestled five world champions.

Today his tremendous experience and wrestling skill are what he uses to guide to triumph the men he manages.

Unlike some other managers, he is known for his sportsmanship and sense of fair play, and has never been known to advise his grapplers to use cruel or rulebreaking tactics to win. His reputation for decency is unquestionable.

"I don't like the way many other managers operate," he says. "They're out for money, which we all are, but I believe we're in a sport and should abide by the rules in everything. They don't abide by any rules and do anything they can to win. We like to win, too, but we like to do it as a sport."

Some of Arnold's opinions have provoked feuds with his less sporting peers, which he handles with the same ease he displayed during his years in the ring. In fact, he settled his rivalry with one of them *in* the ring when he wrestled with the notorious Captain Lou Albano.

"I wrestled Albano in Madison Square Garden. He had been annoying me for so long, and one day, over a year ago, I had won the Manager of the Year trophy, and at the presentation he was mad with envy because he hadn't won it. So he snuck up behind me and struck me over the head with it."

I remark sympathetically that this seems exactly what you would expect from Albano.

When Bob Backlund encountered Ivan Koloff, Skaaland's advice helped him keep the edge. (*Frank Amato*)

The manager of champions—Arnold Skaaland (*Frank Amato*)

Skaaland managed one of the greatest of champions in Bruno Sammartino, here overpowering Blackjack Lanza. (*Frank Amato*)

"Well, I had to even the score," he continues, smiling wryly, "which I did in the ring at Madison Square Garden, before 22,000 people. I annihilated him in about five minutes."

Albano obviously should have known better than to mess with a wrestler like Arnold Skaaland!

Many people believe that Skaaland is really a major force behind the wrestling brilliance of Sammartino and Backlund. I asked him just what he does to help and guide these fighters and keep them at the top.

"I take them to the gym and, for instance, if they're going to wrestle someone like Koloff or Graham, I know how they work. I've wrestled these fellows before, so I know what they do, and I work out with my boys three or four days a week before the fight. I tell them what to look out for and what their opponent's style of wrestling is, and if they get into a predicament how to get out of it. We set up a pattern for how they're going to deal with the fellow."

Managing champions keeps Arnold working and on the road perhaps even more than when he was a grappler. He devotes six to seven days a week to his managerial duties. He unfortunately doesn't have the time to take on many of the new wrestlers who approach him and ask him to manage them.

"I have my hands full," he explains smiling. "I have Bob and Bruno, and we travel all over the world. I'm going constantly. I'm almost never home, one town to another, and it's tough. Then you have to set up a schedule and do all their booking and keep them in shape, make sure they do their roadwork . . ."

I can see how Arnold Skaaland spends his time. He is completely dedicated to the sport and the wrestlers he manages, who are obviously more to him than just fighters in that ring—they are his friends.

"I'm proud of the two boys I have," he says. "I've been with Bruno since the day he started, and he's been a great wrestler, a legend . . . but of all the boys I've seen—and I've traveled all over the world—I don't believe you'll find any better one than Bob Backlund. He's got a lot of wrestling knowledge, and he's unbelievably strong. He's got endurance. He's also a very fine person. I think he's going to go a long way."

A decent grappler, one who knows how to wrestle well and fairly, probably could not ask for a better guide on the way to the top than Arnold Skaaland. Thirty-five years in professional wrestling is quite a foundation to work on.

He is also a good person to ask about how the sport has changed over the years. "I think today the wrestlers are bigger and stronger and faster, through nutrition and better workout conditions. In the old days the guys were really tough, but I don't think they had the same speed and size."

Arnold Skaaland, the wrestler, has set records in that ring which are yet to be broken. And Arnold Skaaland the manager is setting new records every day for skill and sportsmanship that are equally unbeatable. Obviously, for a wrestler today having the name Skaaland behind you means success.

The Grand Wizard of Wrestling

What do Billy and Luke Graham, Crusher Blackwell, and Ernie Ladd all have in common? Yes, well, they are all very aggressive, often vicious, sometimes rulebreaking wrestlers, but that is because they have something else in common—the Grand Wizard of Wrestling. The Wizard explains his management philosophy very simply: "The end justifies the means. I'm a Virgo and I'm a perfectionist," he goes on to say. "It's gonna be done by me and my team, and it's gonna be done 100 percent right or it's not gonna be done. I strive for perfection, I demand it, and I get it."

As a veteran with over 25 years' experience, the Wizard claims to be the senior manager in the sport, and he is known for his driving ambition and his obvious disdain of formal rules. "I don't hesitate to cheat if necessary. I don't hesitate to break a rule here or there. There was never a rule made that wasn't meant to be broken." The Wizard's stable of wrestlers operate on this principle in the ring and obviously feel the same way.

But the Wizard says that his boys aren't always the ones who break the rules. "You will see sometimes the good guy will get away with absolute murder and the referee will not stop him. Referees, though they do a good job and have a very difficult one to do, have a tendency to play up to the fans, they want to be a hero for the fans, and oftentimes they do it at the expense of the so-called villains."

He mentions that frequently the good guy will start punching with his fists, not with his forearms, but no matter how loud the Wizard yells, the referee takes no notice. I'm tempted to point out that whenever I've seen this happen, it's always been because the scientific wrestler has gotten fed up with his rulebreaking opponent's tactics and decided to fight fire with fire. But I knew the Wizard wouldn't see it that way.

The Grand Wizard is one of the few managers in the business who isn't a wrestler himself. He is a short man, and weighs under 155 pounds. Still, he says, he has been physically abused by rivals. "I had my three front teeth knocked out by the five-time world champion, the legendary Lou Thesz—which just goes to show that everything I do, I do with class. They were knocked out by a class man. I also have a scar here on my forehead, when I was pretty well cut up by another person. I have crushed vertebrae in my back. I mean those things do happen to managers. Even skinny managers."

Even though it is rather cruel to attack a man the size of the Wizard, many people would agree that he often provokes such behavior. He has done his best to antagonize such scientific grapplers as Chief Jay Strongbow, Billy White Wolf, and Bruno Sammartino, though these men have used extraordinary restraint in not retaliating.

The Wizard lives in opulence, owns fully staffed mansions, loves fine wines and all the good things in life. His noted stable of wrestlers can certainly provide him with the kind of cash he needs to maintain this high lifestyle. He handles only stars and turns many away.

"I've turned down more than I can take. I

The Grand Wizard of Wrestling is as flamboyant in style
as he is in his choice of dress. (*Frank Amato*)

constantly receive telephone calls from wrestlers wanting me to handle them. But I'm not an easy man to live with really, because I expect the best."

He tells me of one instance in which he dropped a wrestler after only three weeks. "He didn't want to do it my way and he didn't want to discuss it, so we severed the relationship."

He is very proud of all his wrestlers and speaks emphatically about their great styles. Among the most famous, of course, are the Graham family. He originally put Luke and Billy together in tag team competition after Billy lost the WWWF championship, but he is now reconsidering that move. "You see, problem is, they all want that brass ring, the championship belt. It means a lot of money. My plan now for Luke and Billy is to split them up. The team just isn't working, and it must work just the way I want it."

The Wizard has no specific criticism for anyone but Bruno Sammartino. He would like to see him out of the ring permanently.

"I think he should be gracious enough to retire," he says. "He was a great champion, but I think Bruno has passed his mark and he certainly doesn't need the money. I would not like to see him knocked in between the ropes and go out undignified," he concludes, though one might wonder how charitable the Wizard's motives ever are.

The Grand Wizard of Wrestling is certainly not cheered by the fans. The arena rings with boos and jeers whenever the bejeweled turbaned head with those garish sunglasses appears. But never fear—the Wizard feels exactly the same way about them. "Unless

One of the Grand Wizard of Wrestling's "finds" is super-heavyweight Crusher Blackwell, who is here sending Tony Russo down to the mat. (*Frank Amato*)

you plan to print this book on asbestos paper," he sneers, "I don't think I'll say what I'd like to tell the fans. I'll merely say that whatever the fans wish me, I wish them back double." Wrestling fans certainly don't need a crystal ball to understand what the Grand Wizard means by that!

★ 6 ★
Charts on Individual Wrestlers

This section features over 60 of wrestling's top stars, in charts that detail the weight, origin, holds, techniques, titles, and wrestling philosophy of each man. It is meant to expand on the profile section, so that more favorites are featured here than in Chapter Two. Again, I'm sure that some stars will be left out—there is a tremendous number of great mat-men around today and not enough space here to list them all.

Weights, it should be noted, fluctuate tremendously. One grappler explained to me that he could lose about eight pounds during a match! For that reason, the numbers listed here represent averages rather than precise weights.

When I classify a wrestler as "scientific" or as a "rulebreaker," I do not, of course, intend this to be a hard and fast judgment. Some wrestlers admit to breaking or bending rules, some prefer to call their style 'aggressive,' others may change their methods depending on the circumstance. I have used these terms simply to describe a wrestler's reputation with the fans and his fellow wrestlers; they are in no way meant to reflect on their capabilities or wrestling skills.

★
ABDULLAH THE BUTCHER

Khartoum, Sudan
WEIGHT: 285
COMMENTS: Abdullah is a massively built grappler known for his ruthless tactics in the ring. Many people have asked that Abdullah, who has gone berserk on many occasions, be barred from wrestling in their state. He uses whatever tactics (or objects) he has at his disposal to win and has caused many injuries. His matches usually end bloodily, and some grapplers would prefer not to go into the ring with him.

★
ANDRE THE GIANT

Mollien, France
WEIGHT: 472
COMMENTS: At 7 feet 4 inches, Andre the Giant is one of the most awesomely powerful figures in wrestling. He is also one of the most popular, known for his wrestling skill and code of decency. He is undefeated in Battle Royals, and so far no one has been able to pin him. He also has startling speed on his side and opponents tend to use trickery on him, for they are afraid of encountering him head on. He has fought two and three opponents at one time and beaten them easily. Many feel the French giant is *the* unbeatable wrestler.

★
SPIROS ARION

Athens, Greece
WEIGHT: 268
COMMENTS: Once thought to be a great scientific wrestler, the Iron Greek has since become one of the rulebreakers of the sport. He is guided in his shady endeavors by his manager, Fred Blassie. Arion often resorts to kicking and choking, and once he gains an advantage, he will continue to pound his opponent senseless long after it is clear that the match is won.

Andre the Giant (*Frank Amato*)

Bob Backlund vs. Spiros Arion (*Frank Amato*)

★
BOB BACKLUND

Princeton, Minnesota
WEIGHT: 239
COMMENTS: Totally scientific wrestler, schooled in the sport. Backlund uses a combination of speed and incredible strength to defeat opponents. His most devastating move is the atomic kneedrop, but is thoroughly adept in the use of most other holds. Though one of the youngest men in wrestling, he has proved himself as WWWF Heavyweight Champion against some of the roughest men in the sport. He rose to the top of the wrestling world very quickly by taking on any challenger around. His stamina, his capacity for taking punishment, is tremendous. He is well-liked, well-respected, and popular with the crowds.

★
OX BAKER

Indianapolis, Indiana
WEIGHT: 325
COMMENTS: Baker is a big, bulky man, considered by some to be one of the meanest men in the sport. The originator of the deadly heart punch, he has been active in the sport for about 18 years, and his reputation extends around the world. When he goes into the ring, the rulebook goes out. Very agile for his size, Baker can take a lot of punishment—he also tends to continue fighting after the end bell has rung. He is a former boxer and has held many regional wrestling titles. His strength is only average, but his endurance is not; some say that grappling with Baker is like chipping away at marble. He is reputed to have caused serious injuries in the ring.

Crusher Blackwell (*Frank Amato*)

★
CRUSHER BLACKWELL

Stone Mountain, Georgia
WEIGHT: 400
COMMENTS: This huge wrestler from the
Georgia hills displays agility for a man of his
size. He is able to perform flying dropkicks
and dash around the ring when necessary.
He is also cruel with his opponents, fond of
dropping his whole weight upon their necks
or midsections. He is gleeful when someone has been hurt, and he sometimes continues beating his man when he could have
easily made a pin previously. Still, he does
possess good wrestling skills and ability,
and is probably the most active of the super-
heavyweights.

★
NICK BOCKWINKLE

St. Louis, Missouri
WEIGHT: 250
COMMENTS: The AWA champion is totally
under the direction of his manager, Bobby
Heenan, and together they cause havoc in
the ring. Bockwinkle can be extraordinarily
tricky and mean, using any tactic he can to
win. People say he is unimaginative, that he
never improvises, but simply follows the
strategy to the letter that he and Bobby
Heenan have mapped out beforehand. He is
a shrewd fighter who knows how to finish
off an opponent, but his propensity for rulebreaking casts doubts on his true abilities.

★
DINO BRAVO

Montreal, Canada
WEIGHT: 248
COMMENTS: A technically flawless and extremely strong young grappler, previously
part of the WWWF Championship Tag Team.
He finishes off his opponents with extreme
ease in record time, and his speed in the
ring is only equalled by his vast wrestling
knowledge and sense of fair play. He is

Dino Bravo vs. Spiros Arion (*Frank Amato*)

known for expert flying maneuvers, such as the head scissors and the airplane spin, one of his principal finishing holds. He is always pleasant to his fans, and he is a big favorite with them. Many feel he is destined for a championship very shortly. He recently chalked up 69 consecutive victories, all of which he accomplished in less than 15 minutes.

★
JACK BRISCO

Blackwell, Oklahoma
WEIGHT: 232
COMMENTS: Brisco is a true professional who conducts himself with skill and dignity. He held the NWA belt for a considerable time and many feel he could win it back. His specialty is the figure-four leglock, with which he finishes off opponents. He is in excellent physical condition, and for that reason possesses great stamina. He uses both his intelligence and agility in the ring.

★
JIM BRUNZELL

White Bear Lake, Minnesota
WEIGHT: 226
COMMENTS: Brunzell is an excellent young wrestler, destined for superstardom, who once shared the AWA tag team championship with Greg Gagne. He has fine skills and a good analytical mind. He is the master of the Boston crab, which pulls at his opponents' legs and works on the spine. His speed and agility help him to slip out of holds with ease, and he loves to introduce new moves to confound his opponents. He is not afraid of any challenge and is considered a decent man and great sportsman.

★
HAYSTACKS CALHOUN

Morgan's Corner, Arkansas
WEIGHT: 601
COMMENTS: This mammoth super-heavyweight has always been on the side of the good and has often taken brutal punishment for his efforts. His advantage is his size and weight, which enables him to crush against or flatten an opponent for a pin. His lack of speed and difficulty in rising once tossed from the ring have caused some defeats. He is a veteran of the sport who does know wrestling, and though he is not agile, he is an expert at cornering an opponent. He is very popular with the fans and has many friends in pro wrestling.

Haystacks Calhoun vs. Spiros Arion (*George Napolitano*)

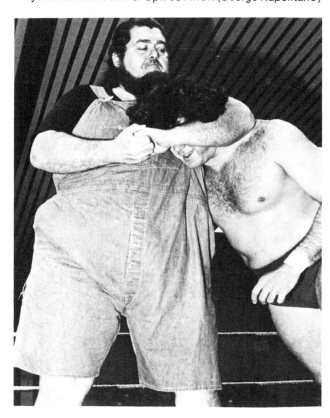

★
THE CRUSHER

Milwaukee, Wisconsin
WEIGHT: 255
COMMENTS: This hero of the working class displays a crude brand of wrestling skill and a rough honesty that endear him to his loyal fans. He has been a top contender in the AWA for many years and has wrestled all the top grapplers in the AWA region. His specialty is close, crunching holds that are geared to cause maximum pain. He is a bitter rival of the Bobby Heenan group of wrestlers and doesn't like the more polished "pretty boys" of the sport.

Domenic DeNucci vs. the Golden Terror (*George Napolitano*)

★
DOMENIC DE NUCCI

Rome, Italy
WEIGHT: 260
COMMENTS: Twice a tag team champion, DeNucci has won many honors in his career in professional wrestling. He is a strong man, an honorable man, a grappler who can take punishment and who can also dish it out when necessary. When he takes to fighting with his fists, it is usually with good cause against a brutal opponent. He is well liked by the fans and other wrestlers, and he uses his experience and strength to good advantage in a threatening situation.

★
BOBBY DUNCUM

Austin, Texas
WEIGHT: 280
COMMENTS: Duncum is a very big man, and a capable athlete who is fast for his size. His style is rough, though, and very aggressive; one of his favorite moves is the Texas bulldozer in which he picks up his man, runs across the ring with him, drops him, and then lands on top of him. He is a young man who has only been wrestling a little over 6 years. He is hot-tempered in the ring and tends to continue battling after the match is over. Because of earlier football injuries, his knees do get hurt in the ring. Managed by Bobby Heenan, he is one of his rough stable of winners.

★
RIC FLAIR

Minneapolis, Minnesota
WEIGHT: 235
COMMENTS: It is hard to assess whether his arrogance or his talent is greater. Flair cer-

Ric Flair (*Frank Amato*)

★
DORY FUNK, JR.

Amarillo, Texas
WEIGHT: 245
COMMENTS: The ex-NWA champion, son of Dory Funk. Unlike his brother Terry, he controls his temper and relies on a precise, well thought-out strategy. He spends a lot of time training and refining his moves, and he is a very proud sportsman, conscious of his family's tradition in the arena. He is able to attack an opponent aggressively when the need arises, and can take a lot of punishment and still go on to victory.

Dory Funk, Jr. (*George Napolitano*)

tainly has enough strength and wrestling skill, but he seems to prefer brutal, punishing tactics. He tries to get away with as much as he can in the ring and boasts about it afterwards. His great attribute is speed, which he uses well, and his atomic neckbreaker and flying kneedrop are also keys to his success. He is tough and can take a lot in the ring, but opponents who face him are aware that he may cause them some crippling injury. Though not liked for his tactics, he has a large and loyal following and is a real crowd-drawer for his unexpected moves and his flamboyant costuming and style. He was trained under the guidance of Verne Gagne in the beginning, before he turned so aggressive, and some wrestlers feel that he is among the most talented young men in the sport.

★
TERRY FUNK

Amarillo, Texas
WEIGHT: 238
COMMENTS: Another ex-NWA champion from the Funk family. He prefers more questionable tactics than his father and brother do, and does not often lean toward scientific maneuvers. His short temper often gets him disqualified; he is a dangerous man who can match brutality with the most vehement of rulebreakers. His spinning toe hold is a devastating finishing move. He has recently appeared in Sylvester Stallone's movie, *Paradise Alley,* as Frankie the Thumper.

★
GREG GAGNE

Mound, Minnesota
WEIGHT: 219
COMMENTS: Like his famous father, Greg Gagne believes in clean, scientific tactics. He is very light, but he has a lot of speed and is innovative with his hold and maneuvers. He enjoys challenges and loves to improvise with new moves to meet them. He is one of the most scientifically oriented of all young wrestlers and is fanatic about staying in prime physical shape. His stamina and courage are very impressive.

★
VERNE GAGNE

Minneapolis, Minnesota
WEIGHT: 230
COMMENTS: The ex-AWA champion is recognized by many as the dean of scientific wrestling. Over his thirty-year career he has always been at the top and has done much to help the sport and to encourage young wrestlers. Once an Olympic wrestler, he possesses a tremendous amount of skill and stays in shape by constant training. His sleeper hold is still his most devastating weapon. He is a very intelligent man, and he uses that precision in the ring. He has astonishing stamina and a fine ability to think clearly and keep his temper in check.

★
TONY GAREA

Auckland, New Zealand
WEIGHT: 240
COMMENTS: Garea is quick, strong, and young, a very talented grappler who has defeated some of wrestling's toughest opponents. He is knowledgeable with his holds, and his use of the abdominal stretch is powerful, a hold he will not release even when both grapplers have toppled to the mat. He is a decent man, popular with his fans. He does lose his temper with ruthless opponents, which has occasionally cost him a match. Shared WWWF Tag Team Championship with his good friend Larry Zbyszko.

★
SUPERSTAR BILLY GRAHAM

Paradise Valley, Arizona
WEIGHT: 270
COMMENTS: The ex-WWWF Champion is as colorful and boastful as he is ruthless. A man of tremendous strength, a fanatical trainer with an impressive physique, he is a member of the famous Graham family of wrestlers. He is arrogant, and has been involved in many bitter rivalries with other wrestlers. Because of his strength, his

Superstar Billy Graham vs. Chief Jay Strongbow (*Frank Amato*)

bearhugs, spinebreakers, and abdominal stretches are devastating. Claims his title was stolen from him, though many people feel he won the belt illegally himself from Bruno Sammartino. Will resort to illegal tactics galore when things are not going his way, and he is universally feared for his brutality.

breaks of brutality and rulebreaking, he can seem to go berserk on his opponent and pummel him to a point of no return. His taped thumb finds its way into many grapplers' throats, and he has been known to smuggle objects into the ring concealed in his trunks. He is a large, powerful man, but does seem to run out of courage when similarly attacked.

★
LUKE GRAHAM

Atlanta, Georgia
WEIGHT: 291
COMMENTS: Older half-brother of Billy Graham, Luke is a veteran of the mat. Known by fans as "Crazy Luke" because of his out-

★
CHAVO GUERRERO

El Paso, Texas
WEIGHT: 215
COMMENTS: Chavo is quite light for a heavyweight, is really more of a junior heavy-

Chavo Guerrero (*Frank Amato*)

broke Bruno Sammartino's neck seems to delight in crippling opponents. His feared lariat hold and padded elbow are what did Bruno and so many others in. He does possess enormous strength and has bested grapplers all over the world. He is a methodical wrestler with a lot of stamina, but his aggressive tactics sometimes obscure his skill. In tag team competition he has been known to turn on his partners.

Stan Hansen (*George Napolitano*)

weight, but incredibly strong. His father was Gory Guerrero. He is a fan's favorite in Los Angeles and San Diego and is known for his aerial maneuvers, dropkicks, flying head scissors, and reliance on speed. He is not big or powerfully built, but relies on the scientific style he started with a few years ago. His lack of size leaves him open at times to larger opponents.

★
STAN HANSEN

Canyon, Texas
WEIGHT: 310
COMMENTS: The wrestler from Texas who will forever be remembered as the man who

Lord Alfred Hayes vs. Gino Hernandez (*George Napolitano*)

★
LORD ALFRED HAYES

Windemere, England
WEIGHT: 235
COMMENTS: Hayes is small, but he makes up for it with his scientific skill and his intelligence and composure in the ring. He excels at his one specialty hold, London Bridge, a forceful variation of the half nelson which brings his opponents helplessly down to the mat. As a manager, he gets angry easily when other wrestlers are going after his boys, or in some cases, trying to unmask them (as with Super Destroyer II). His greatest asset is his speed.

★
GINO HERNANDEZ

Houston, Texas
WEIGHT: 239
COMMENTS: Gino used to be a favorite with the fans, but in the last year he has turned more to rulebreaking and roughhousing. He was popular in Detroit and later in Texas, where his father, Louis Hernandez, was also a wrestler. He is very fast, but slender and not that tall—about six foot one. He is managed by Gary Hart. Gino is also known for his short temper in the ring, which provokes his aggressive attacks on opponents.

★
ROCKY JOHNSON

San Francisco, California
WEIGHT: 253
COMMENTS: Johnson is an outstanding scientific wrestler, a credit to the sport. He has taken severe beatings in the ring and still gone on to triumph. When enraged, he can be as ruthless as anyone, but he tries to stay calm and level-headed. His speed helps him tremendously, since he really can't compete with many other wrestlers in strength and power. He is very popular and is polite and respectful toward everyone. Some believe he doesn't have enough fire in him to win a major belt.

Rocky Johnson vs. Roger Kirby (*Frank Amato*)

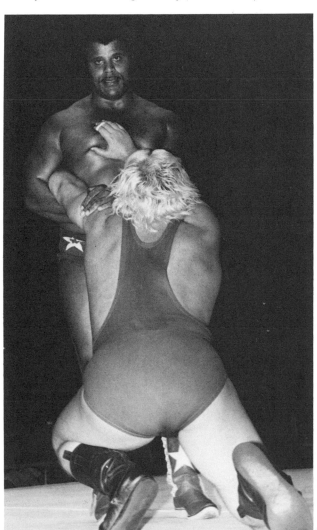

Paul Jones (*Frank Amato*)

★
PAUL JONES

Port Arthur, Texas
WEIGHT: 230
COMMENTS: Jones is a big talent who can handle both scientific wrestlers and rule-breakers. He has held major regional titles but never a world belt. His sleeper hold and spinebreaker are devastating moves, and he is a methodical man who carefully plans out his strategy before a match. He has tremendous strength and agility and rarely loses his cool.

★
S.D. JONES

Philadelphia, Pennsylvania
WEIGHT: 246
COMMENTS: "Special Delivery" Jones is a tough man to get down in the ring, for he can take a lot of punishment and also dish it out. He is a kind and clean man, basically a scientific wrestler, but he can become enraged at a beating he is undergoing and turn the tide with his skill and strength. His head butts usually leave his opponents semiconscious.

★
IVAN KOLOFF

Moscow, Russia
WEIGHT: 263
COMMENTS: Though many view him as one of the most ruthless fighters in the ring, he is also widely considered one of the most skillful. An ex-WWWF Champion, who, under the guidance of manager Lou Albano, has resorted to cruelty and ruthlessness even when he could win easily without it. His strength, seen in his crushing bearhug, is phenomenal; so is his agility and his confident skill. The Russian Bear is not short on courage, though some feel that he tortures opponents for the sheer delight of it.

★
KILLER KARL KOX

Amarillo, Texas
WEIGHT: 250
COMMENTS: Known throughout Florida for his rough, aggressive tactics. He is not popular with the fans because of his brutality and rulebreaking; he is known as Crippler Karl Kox, or Killer Kox. People say he goes out of his way to hurt someone

Killer Karl Kox vs. Rocky Johnson (*George Napolitano*)

when it is not at all necessary, and continues to attack after the bout is over.

★
KILLER KRUPP

Mannheim, Germany
WEIGHT: 256
COMMENTS: A very recent attraction in Texas, as a very rough rulebreaking type. His specialties are claw holds—face claws, stomach claws, arm claws, eye claws; he is also fond of reaching under the armpits and clawing there. The fans hate him, but come to jeer, and to support his sometimes hapless opponents. Krupp has been known to refuse to break a claw hold even after the match is over.

★
ERNIE LADD

Houston, Texas
WEIGHT: 315
COMMENTS: The Big Cat, all 6 foot 9 inches of him, is a former football player who was once thought to be an unbeatable scientific wrestler. However, under the hand of his manager, the Grand Wizard, Ladd has changed to a grappler who throws away the rulebook. His enormous size, tricky maneuvers, strength, and speed make him truly fearsome and his taped karate thumb thrust to the neck has left many an opponent struggling and gasping for air at his feet, which are always ready to deliver a kick. He would like a major belt or at least to see the defeat of his rival, Andre the Giant.

★
PETER MAIVIA

Samoa

WEIGHT: 270

COMMENTS: Maivia was a popular favorite, known for his skill, agility, and a powerful body that could take the blows of the roughest opponents. He has suddenly turned on his former friends, betrayed them in tag team matches, and gone over to the camp of manager Fred Blassie, complete with all those questionable tactics. Because he still possesses the astonishing skills he had before this change in philosophy, he is considered to be a truly dangerous man.

High Chief Peter Maivia vs. Superstar Billy Graham (*Frank Amato*)

★
MIL MASCARAS

Mexico City, Mexico

WEIGHT: 240

COMMENTS: Considered the greatest "flying wrestler" in the ring because of his quick aerial kicks and maneuvers, Mascaras is also thought to be the greatest scientific wrestler by many because of his great repertory of moves. He owns a thousand masks, and he is never seen without one; he is also known for his colorful costumes. He varies his maneuvers so often that opponents are confounded and his catlike grace prevents them from getting a solid grip on him. A highly ethical and decent man, his code of honor both in and out of the ring is legendary. His two brothers are also masked wrestlers, and Mascaras is a movie star in his native Mexico.

★
MASKED SUPERSTAR

Singapore

WEIGHT: 280

COMMENTS: This grappler began wrestling in Singapore, and then came to the United States by way of Canada. He is very fast for his size and has some excellent moves. With the help of his former manager, Lord Alfred Hayes, he learned a variety of European holds. He is a rough customer who loses his temper in the ring and can be brutal. He does have a habit of looking away from his opponent, and his opponents have often taken advantage of this. He is said to use well-programmed strategy rather than improvisation. Though aggressive, he is not very violent.

Wahoo McDaniel (*George Napolitano*)

★
WAHOO McDANIEL

McAlester, Oklahoma

WEIGHT: 260

COMMENTS: McDaniel's early fame came in pro football, where he was a top player. He has a stocky build, but is very fast for his size, due to his athletic background. He carries his size well, and is a great scientific wrestler, well versed in the grappling principles of balance and leverage. He is willing to get rough if he has to, has had some heated rivalries with people like Greg Valentine, but he is not easily provoked. He is a very colorful, well-loved, and talented wrestler.

★
GORILLA MONSOON

Rochester, New York

WEIGHT: 401

COMMENTS: A veteran of the ring, his great battles with Bruno Sammartino have made wrestling history. He is a huge man, 6 feet 7 inches tall, and he uses his tremendous power skillfully. His years of experience make him a rough opponent, and he finishes off opponents with a succession of judo and karate chops. He was once a genuine villain, but he saw the light and is now a decent scientific grappler, and is always friendly and helpful to fans.

★
ANGELO MOSCA

Edmonton, Canada

WEIGHT: 315

COMMENTS: The Georgia Heavyweight Champion is nicknamed "King Kong" for his awesome power in the ring. He is a notorious rulebreaker who has brutally crushed many foes, and he uses his finishing move, the elbow smash, even on helpless opponents. His peculiar charm has attracted many fans and some feel he is a future world champion.

Angelo Mosca vs. the Avenger (*George Napolitano*)

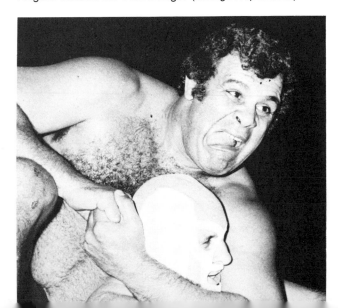

★
MR. WRESTLING I

Atlanta, Georgia

WEIGHT: 235

COMMENTS: The original Mr. Wrestling, Tim Woods is a masked grappler who has considerable scientific skills. He is capable of mastering any situation that may arise in the ring. He has had major feuds with many wrestlers—among them Abdullah the Butcher, Jerry Lawler, and Ole and Gene Anderson. He almost always keeps his cool, and composure plus solid wrestling ability is usually enough to win.

★
MR. WRESTLING II

(Undisclosed Origin)

WEIGHT: 232

COMMENTS: This masked man is a decent, skillful contender in the ring, loved by his fans and admired for his versatility by his colleagues. He has taken many brutal beatings at the hands of foes like Abdullah, but his strength has never deserted him. He has a strict code of sporting decency and is ashamed when he loses his temper in a rough match. He is steady and effective, rather than flashy, and his headlock and the judo holds he has mastered are the chief weapons in his arsenal. He is very proud of the tradition behind his mask.

★
BLACKJACK MULLIGAN

San Antonio, Texas

WEIGHT: 320

COMMENTS: Mulligan has a reputation for savagery throughout the sport. He can use either legal or illegal tactics, has a wide range of moves in each, but his actions usually end up questionable. He is a large man with a great deal of strength, but not much speed. He is unpredictable in that ring, one minute fighting fair and the next exploding into aggressiveness. One of the most feared men in the sport.

★
DICK MURDOCH

Waxahachie, Texas

WEIGHT: 260

COMMENTS: People see Murdoch as a contender for the NWA title, after his capture of the Missouri State Championship. He has a wide repertoire of moves, much skill, but is short on speed. Once possessed of a terrible temper, he controls it more often now. He was Dusty Rhodes's tag team partner, when they were called "The Outlaws."

★
KEN PATERA

Portland, Oregon

WEIGHT: 275

COMMENTS: An Olympic medalist in weight-lifting, considered by many to be the

Ken Patera vs. Mil Mascaras (*Frank Amato*)

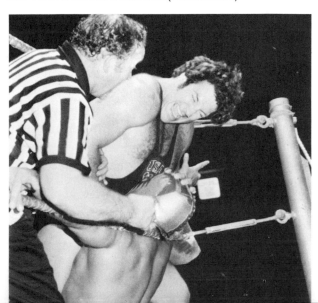

CHARTS ON INDIVIDUAL WRESTLERS

strongest man in the sport, Patera started out as a scientific wrestler, but he is now feared and hated by fans and other grapplers. His swinging neckbreaker has put Billy White Wolf, among others, in the hospital. He clamps on that hold for much longer than he should. Once barred from the East Coast for his brutal tactics, Patera now holds sway in the Mid-Atlantic. He was managed by Lou Albano, who seemed to encourage this shady application of the man's phenomenal strength.

Pat Patterson (*Frank Amato*)

★
PAT PATTERSON

Los Angeles, California
WEIGHT: 240
COMMENTS: Patterson is a skillful grappler, now teamed up with Ray Stevens, whose

tactics seem to vacillate between scientific expertise and rulebending. He and Stevens are known for the "bombs away" maneuver, which begins with a leap from the top rope. He has a great deal of stamina and can fight clean or dirty as the occasion demands. People say that the partners' combined experience and thorough knowledge of the sport makes them an unbeatable wrestling duo.

★
IVAN PUTSKI

Krakow, Poland
WEIGHT: 240
COMMENTS: Putski, the Polish Power, is a beloved favorite, an incredibly strong man with a well-kept muscular physique. Though he is a scientific expert, he will lose his temper with a vicious adversary and let loose as savagely as anyone. His love for his fans and his good will toward people is well known, as are his fierce competitiveness, incredible stamina, and wrestling ability. His headlocks are devastating, when combined with that awesome strength. For a smaller man (5 feet 10 inches) he is able to challenge and win over much larger opponents due to his drive.

★
HARLEY RACE

Kansas City, Missouri
WEIGHT: 248
COMMENTS: Twice NWA champion, Harley Race is a grappler who has years of wrestling experience behind him, but doesn't always use it fairly. Though he does use unnecessary violence in his matches, he also

Harley Race vs. Rocky Johnson (*Frank Amato*)

shows a great deal of skill, and takes on any-one who wishes to challenge him, thereby giving newcomers a chance to prove them-selves. He is agile and strong, and his use of the piledriver has finished off many of these challengers.

★
BARON VON RASCHKE

Germany
WEIGHT: 265
COMMENTS: This rigid and harsh German is known for his ruthlessness in the ring and his unpredictable style. He has a vast ama-teur background and solid skills, but can easily turn in the middle of a match to being extremely aggressive. He was the Missouri Champion, U.S. Champion and European Champion, to name just a few of his titles. He is a large, fearsome-looking man, and marches into the ring like a general march-ing into battle. Von Raschke is very agile, quick, with good reflexes and counters; he perfected his backbreaker, which he calls the hangman. His chief ring rivalries have been with such grapplers as Jack Brisco and Pedro Morales. His finishing hold—the claw—had damaged quite a few opponents.

CHARTS ON INDIVIDUAL WRESTLERS

Baron von Raschke (*Frank Amato*)

geous style have made him unforgettable. He is basically a decent wrestler, but can brawl and attack with the best. His "bionic elbow" has caused many a pin. Some question his actual ability, but his stamina and intensely individualistic personality will drive him to victory when all else fails.

Dusty Rhodes (*Frank Amato*)

★
DUSTY RHODES

Austin, Texas
WEIGHT: 265
COMMENTS: Definitely one of the most popular wrestlers in the sport, the flamboyant Texan fights all over the country and the world, and never turns down a challenge. He is a master of bloody matches, including the Texas Bull-Rope, and is known to bleed and take it. His incredible costumes and outra-

★
VICTOR RIVERA

Puerto Rico
WEIGHT: 253
COMMENTS: Rivera was another one of those great scientific wrestlers turned rulebreaker under the guidance of his manager, Fred Blassie. Once a man with great speed, skill and strength, Rivera now uses those qualities to batter opponents, even after they have fallen from the ring, and his kicks have left their marks in the side of many helpless grapplers.

★
BILLY ROBINSON

Manchester, England
WEIGHT: 250
COMMENTS: This gracious gentleman from Great Britain always exhibits breeding, class, and control in the ring. He has taught and helped many wrestlers on their way up and is often considered to be one of the most skillful men in the sport. He has great speed, awesome strength, and has mastered numerous complex moves, including the suplex. He would like to win a title, but somehow it has always eluded him.

Billy Robinson (*Frank Amato*)

★
JOHNNY RODZ

New York City
WEIGHT: 240
COMMENTS: The "Unpredictable" Johnny Rodz is just that—surprising his opponents with his speed and his wide array of legal and questionable maneuvers. He becomes furiously competitive as soon as he steps into the ring and will use any combination to win. He is fond of jumping off the top ropes onto the backs of his opponents or pounding them mercilessly. His agility is astonishing and he can withstand a lot of punishment.

★
BRUNO SAMMARTINO

Abruzzi, Italy
WEIGHT: 255
COMMENTS: The "Living Legend" of professional wrestling, Bruno Sammartino, held the WWWF belt for a period that spanned 14 years. He is best known for his remarkable strength and endurance, and his fearlessness when facing the most brutal of adversaries. Probably one of the most popular wrestlers who ever lived, Bruno cares deeply for his fans and has done a lot of charitable work. He has solid scientific powers, but he is also known for strong aggressiveness when set upon by a rampant rulebreaker.

Baron Mikel Scicluna (*Frank Amato*)

CHARTS ON INDIVIDUAL WRESTLERS

★
BARON MIKEL SCICLUNA

Malta
WEIGHT: 265
COMMENTS: Scicluna is a large, powerfully built man who often resorts to rather questionable tactics in the ring. He will leave the ring to escape further punishment, but doesn't mind inflicting it on an opponent. Though his strength and stamina are great, his reflexes are sometimes not as quick as they might be. He does pose a formidable threat to any wrestler who meets him.

★
THE SHEIK

Lebanon
WEIGHT: 250
COMMENTS: The mystery man from the Middle East has almost become legendary for his rulebreaking and all-around brutality. He has used devices such as pencils and fire to maim and blind opponents. Many are afraid of getting into the ring with him, knowing some severe injury will be the result. He speaks only Arabic and is usually accompanied by his loyal manager, Abdullah Farouk. It is said that he is endowed with powers from Allah, although others refute this, saying that his only powers lie in his trickery. But the Sheik does have solid wrestling skills which he does exhibit on occasion and can match holds when he chooses to.

★
ALEXI SMIRNOFF

Moscow, Russia
WEIGHT: 254
COMMENTS: Smirnoff started out as a scientific wrestler, but changed his style to that of rulebreaking, though he is not the kind to use foreign objects in the ring. He is versatile, though he relies heavily on six basic holds. He gets angry in the ring, and can get rather heated and vocal. His wrestling experience was in Canada, and some say he lacks experience in the more open style of United States wrestling.

★
STAN STASIAK

Buzzard Creek, Oregon
WEIGHT: 272
COMMENTS: Former WWWF champion Stasiak is known chiefly for his heart punch—that deadly fist to the chest which overcomes most opponents. Lately, however, the heart punch has been missing its target more and more, though Stasiak says he has just learned how to "improve it." He is known for his aggressive, rulebreaking tactics, which have caused many a scientific wrestler to lose his temper. He is powerful rather than fast, and he does have wrestling ability.

★
RICK STEAMBOAT

Honolulu, Hawaii
WEIGHT: 232
COMMENTS: This good-looking young grappler has risen to the top professional rankings and the popularity lists in a very short time, and is now considered a top contender for the NWA belt. He is involved in a bitter feud with Ric Flair, and the United States Belt passes regularly back and forth between them. He has youth, power, endurance and agility on his side, along with de-

cency and scientific skill. He thought of quitting after receiving incredibly rough treatment at the hands of foes, but his loyal fans persuaded him to continue.

★
GEORGE "THE ANIMAL" STEELE

Detrcit, Michigan
WEIGHT: 270
COMMENTS: This maniacal grappler rarely uses anything remotely resembling scientific technique. He is a huge, powerful man who sports a green tongue and an insane look, drools, and uses any kind of viciousness he can conceive to do in his opponent. He is slow but brutal, known to use objects and illegal maneuvers galore, and torments grapplers even after he has won the match. Even his manager, Lou Albano, says he is a hard man to control. Many wrestlers cite him as the most vicious and unpredictable of all.

George "the Animal" Steele vs. High Chief Peter Maivia (*Frank Amato*)

Ray Stevens (*Frank Amato*)

★
RAY STEVENS

San Francisco, California
WEIGHT: 255
COMMENTS: Ray Stevens is a former rulebreaker who changed his ways after a feud with the Bobby Heenan tribe, though he sometimes forgets himself and earns a disqualification. He and Nick Bockwinkle were the AWA tag team with the longest championship reign; he teams with Pat Patterson with the same belt. He is thought of by many as a "natural" wrestler, a man who has

CHARTS ON INDIVIDUAL WRESTLERS

excellent abilities in that ring, and doesn't have to really dwell on what he's doing to be victorious. His "bombs away" jump from the top rope has finished many off, as has his cleverness and agility. He doesn't rely on prematch strategy, preferring improvisation in the ring.

★
CHIEF JAY STRONGBOW

Pawhuska, Oklahoma
WEIGHT: 255
COMMENTS: The fearless Indian warrior has been engaged in many rough battles and many feuds and has usually come out triumphant. His costume and ceremonial headdress is a legend, as is his war dance, which he uses to summon up his strength. A decent and fine grappler, he often has to fight fire with fire when attacked by brutal opponents. He held the WWWF tag team championship with Billy White Wolf until White Wolf was hospitalized by Ken Patera. His famous sleeper hold has put many men out and given Strongbow an easy victory. He is intensely loyal to his fans and his friends.

★
SUPER DESTROYER

Gibraltar
WEIGHT: 270
COMMENTS: The Super Destroyer varies in weight from 270 to over 300 pounds—he is a very tall man, and very powerful. He doesn't observe the rules particularly strictly and he is very versatile in his maneuvers. His opponent rarely knows what the Destroyer is going to do next. He has been managed by both Gary Hart and Lord Alfred Hayes. He is

a masked grappler, and his opponents sometimes try to twist that mask, so that he can't see. Because of sweat under the mask, he sometimes loses peripheral vision, and a small, fast man can give him a rough time, because of his lack of speed.

★
STEVE TRAVIS

Charlottesville, Virginia
WEIGHT: 245
COMMENTS: Travis, a newcomer who has proven his abilities first in the NWA regions, was elected Rookie of the Year in the WWWF for 1979. He is a talented scientific athlete, an ex-football player who demonstrates a lot of stamina and a solid knowledge of wrestling holds. Though he has been wrestling professionally for just three years, his courage and ability to withstand punishment will often win him a match where his experience would not have. Favors suplexes, dropkicks; he is very agile and lean. Very popular with his fans and many feel he has a promising career ahead of him.

★
GREG VALENTINE

Seattle, Washington
WEIGHT: 240
COMMENTS: Valentine has been accused of purposely devising methods to torture his opponents and of being utterly ruthless in the ring. He teams up on occasion with Ric Flair, though people wonder how they can trust each other. He possesses adequate speed, and he is exceptionally strong. His flying atomic skullcrusher is said to have

Greg Valentine vs. El Olympico (*George Napolitano*)

caused brain damage in several of his opponents. His knowledge of moves and maneuvers may be underrated. He is also known for his figure-four leglock, which has temporarily crippled many opponents.

★
LARRY ZBYSZKO

Pittsburgh, Pennsylvania
WEIGHT: 250
COMMENTS: Once known as a protégé of Bruno Sammartino, Larry has proven over the years that he is a wrestler of such high caliber he can stand on his own. His advantages lie in his wrestling skills and agility, and his speed and quick thinking. He is loyal to his fans and his friends, and is known to be an excellent and reliable tag team partner. Many people feel he cannot fail to become a world champion. His decency and high sense of sportsmanship are very important to him.

★ Index ★

INDEX